MW00378019

CLASSIC RAILROAD SCENES

43 years of rare color photos

ART PETERSON

Kalmbach Media

Kalmbach Books
(A division of Kalmbach Media)
21027 Crossroads Circle
Waukesha, Wisconsin 53186
www.KalmbachHobbyStore.com

Published in 2019
23 22 21 20 19   1 2 3 4 5

Manufactured in China

ISBN: 978-1-62700-609-5
EISBN: 978-1-62700-610-1

Editor: Eric White
Book Design: Lisa Bergman

Library of Congress Control Number: 2018963857

INTRODUCTION

I can't remember a time when I wasn't fascinated by trains. They conveyed size and power in every way: whether it was the hum of gears on an L train, the way a Chicago & North Western Baby Train Master towered over a small boy, or the blast from an approaching air horn, every aspect caught my attention. Over time, other facets of railroading drew me in: why the New York, Ontario & Western was unable to succeed, let alone survive; what it must have been like to hack the Pennsylvania main line out of the mountain wilderness in the 1850s; or discovering the personalities that shaped the various railroads, outsized-egos and all.

Every picture tells a story, and each photographer approaches a subject in his or her own unique way. Collecting the work of multiple photographers has always appealed to me, and I now have several hundred thousand railroading images. The work of more than 25 photographers is included in this book. Sadly, many of the color slides have no name on their mounts, so the camera work remains unattributed. Railfanning can be a community activity, and certainly determining locations for many of these images required the assistance of a lot of extremely knowledgeable fans. Those folks are listed in the acknowledgments, and I owe each of them a huge debt of thanks for their patience with my questions and for the information they shared. I hope the resulting descriptions go beyond the obvious and serve to stimulate your interest in the subjects shown.

Availability and cost kept many photographers from going the color film route in the late 1930s/early 1940s. Some, sadly, experimented with unstable films or also-ran products. Happily, there were a few pioneers who converted early to Kodachrome and stuck with it. Names like Frank Butts or Barney Stone are in this group. Their travels also took them to many places off the beaten track, allowing them to record some unique perspectives of the daily operations on America's railroads and transit lines.

The rail world was undergoing dramatic change: rail industry track-miles had peaked in 1916 and declined by 5 percent by 1940. Even more dramatically, 55 percent of streetcar track-miles had disappeared by 1940. A staggering 75 percent of interurban track-miles were gone by the time the first images in this book were exposed.

With each abandonment, train-off or bus replacement, another opportunity for recording those once-typical scenes would be lost. And though our photographers couldn't know it at the time, the coming war, the post-war prosperity, and the following decades would have profound impacts on society and how Americans enjoyed their leisure time. The pull of "downtown" would diminish and the character of those cities would be transformed as the years passed. The debt we owe these photographers for taking the time to compose these shots and record them for all to enjoy is monumental.

ILLINOIS POWER & LIGHT NO. 470

Adams Street, Peoria, Illinois | circa 1940

The location is Adams and Franklin in Peoria circa 1940, based on license plate color. You won't find this intersection on today's maps: ramps to and from I-40 are just one project that has transformed this area. All the buildings in the block to the right of the approaching Illinois Power & Light Birney are gone. You have to go back a block north to Harrison, where the building that then housed Cohen's is still standing. Some of the advertised firms in this view were Peoria institutions—Merkel & Sons shows up in turn-of-the-century views, while Rue Seeds was advertising its seeds and products in the 1920s. Increased disposable income in the 1920s led to a greater than ten-fold explosion in advertising expenditures. Proctor & Gamble began implementing the brand management marketing concept from 1931. Neon signs first appeared in the United States at a Los Angeles-area Packard dealership in the early 1920s.

R. V. Mehlenbeck photo

7

CHICAGO, INDIANAPOLIS & LOUISVILLE (MONON) NO. 444

Fifth Street, Lafayette, Indiana | March 14, 1940

Frank Butts and John Humiston (caught in the act of photographing CI&L Train 5) made the trek to Lafayette to shoot the last day of the city's streetcar operation. Taking the opportunity to shoot the midday train to Louisville as it moved down the middle of Fifth Street, this image captures the Monon passenger service in the era before John Barriger, F3s, and ex-Army hospital cars transformed it. Chicago, Indianapolis & Louisville Pacific No. 444, built by Alco in January 1923, heads the train, and immediately behind it is one of the Barney & Smith 1913-vintage baggage-RPOs. At this time, the average age of the Monon passenger cars was 25 years old, with the oldest active car being an 1893 Ohio Falls Car Company (later merged into ACF) baggage car. The newest was also a baggage car—a 1929 Pullman product.

F. E. Butts photo

MISSOURI & KANSAS NO. 118

Park and Cherry, Olathe, Kansas | March 1940

William B. Strang platted the town of Overland Park, Kansas, built the Missouri & Kansas Railway, and built an airfield in Overland Park, which saw its first public flight in 1909. The M&K began operations with the Strang gas-electric railcar in 1907, but was converted to electric operation by 1909. Brill subsidiary American Car Co. built five wood-steel cars for the M&K in two orders, delivered in 1908 and 1909. A 1925 fire at the line's Overland Park carhouse destroyed several cars. Missouri & Kansas turned to American Car for three lightweight, one-man cars to offset its loss and converted its surviving older cars to one-man operation. Rebuilt No. 118, renumbered on top of the lightweights, is shown westbound on Park at Cherry in Olathe in March 1940. All service ended on July 24, 1940. Both Olathe and Lenexa commemorate the line with a Strang Line Road.

F. E. Butts photo

11

Sand Springs Railway No. 66

Main and Broadway, Sand Springs, Oklahoma | March 23, 1940

Often, a dominant figure provided the impetus for social change, industrial development, and transportation improvements. Sand Springs, Oklahoma, and Anaconda, Montana, (page 72) are examples in this book. Sand Springs, and the railway connecting it to Tulsa, were all the work of one man, Charles Page. Commensurate with this status, a statue of Mr. Page (at right) keeps watch from the town commons.

This experimental philanthropic community and planned industrial development located the industrial park to the south and the residential area north. The railway was essential for the industrial development and opened in 1911, but it was not electrified until the following year. The philanthropic component, the Sand Springs Home, opened in 1917. Sand Springs Railway car 66, skirting the commons on March 23, 1940, was one of seven pioneering lightweight (26,000-pound) interurban cars the Cincinnati Car Co. had built for the Cincinnati, Lawrenceburg & Aurora. These cars were sold to Sand Springs through an equipment dealer in 1932.

F. E. Butts photo

UNION ELECTRIC RAILWAY NO. 71

Walnut and Eighth, Coffeyville, Kansas | March 23, 1940

Union Traction Co. of Kansas was one of those improbable survivors. Incorporated in January 1904, the interurban was operating between Coffeyville and Independence by July 1907, and extended its route north to Parsons by December 1912. A line from Coffeyville to Nowata, Oklahoma, began operating in 1914, less than a decade after Oklahoma had been admitted to the Union. Bankrupt in 1927, the operation was reorganized as Union Electric Railway a decade later. Single- and double-truck Birneys were used to economize the service, and car 71 is shown southbound on Walnut at Eighth in Coffeyville in late March 1940. Union Electric Railway was famous for the hand-lettered dash signs proclaiming its "Deep-Cut Fares" and for its minimal physical plant. Despite this, UER handled decent freight traffic and survived intact into June 1947. The Coffeyville interurban station building still stands today.

F. E. Butts photo

15

ST. LOUIS PUBLIC SERVICE NO. 1136

Kingsland and Delmar, St. Louis, Missouri | September 1, 1940

United Railways Co. had opened its sprawling 39th and Park shop complex in 1903, and like most major streetcar shops of the day, this facility was fully capable of building and rebuilding streetcars in addition to looking after the "care and feeding" of the fleet. Car 1136 was built in those shops in 1911. In this September 1940 view, it has completed a trip on the 5/Creve Coeur Lake line, leaving the center reservation on Kingsland near Delmar. Several riders are making connections to a Midland Motor Bus Yellow Coach (at the curb) that will head to Wellston or to a St. Louis Public Service Delmar line car, which is one of the then-brand-new PCC cars. Today, this location is a block north of the Delmar-Kingsland terminal of the Loop Trolley Line, which will connect the Delmar Loop to the Missouri History Museum in Forest Park.

R. V. Mehlenbeck photo

16

17

Third Avenue Railway System No. 1096

42nd Street and Fifth Avenue, New York, New York | circa 1942

The significant 42nd Street crosstown route in Manhattan came under the control of the Third Avenue Railway System in 1896 and was electrified between 1898 and 1901. Brill developed its semi-convertible car design around 1902. Car 1096 is part of a 200-car order TARS placed in January 1909. The first of these cars was received in New York City just five months later.

To the left of the westbound car is the 500 Fifth Avenue Building, a 60-story Art Deco structure that was completed in 1930. In this 1942 view, note the Santa Fe and North Western logos on the second- and third-story office windows, respectively. Both roads had a significant presence in their offices, including general agents, district passenger agents, and eastern perishable agents. As for the 42nd Street car line, it would survive the transition to the Third Avenue Transit System in 1943, and buses would take the place of the streetcars in mid-November 1946.

B. L. Stone photo

19

CONNECTICUT CO. NO. 1474

Broadway Station, New Haven, Connecticut | August 8, 1942

The New Haven Railroad first acquired control of the streetcar lines in New Haven in mid-1904. At first, the operation was under the Consolidated Railway banner, but this evolved into the Connecticut Co., formed on May 31, 1907. Antitrust concerns saw the company turned over to a voting trusteeship, but control by the railroad was restored in 1925. The New Haven's bankruptcy in 1935 led to the sale of assets to a local power company. The familiar yellow-orange open cars hung on in New Haven until September 25, 1948. They were ideal for quick loading and unloading of the crowds at the Yale Bowl or at area amusement parks. World War II interrupted plans for conversion. In the postwar era, the city, local merchants, and the operating company agreed to a complete change of downtown traffic patterns, which led to the end of streetcar service. The Broadway median was a casualty of this conversion, being given over to automobile parking.

B. L. Stone photo

OKLAHOMA RAILWAYS NO. 122

Main Street, Oklahoma City, Oklahoma | December 1945

Glories of Christmas Past—Oklahoma Railways city car 122 heads west on Main Street near Hudson in Oklahoma City in December 1945. The downtown merchants joined in to ensure that this Christmas would be restored to its prewar grandeur. As was common with many U.S. cities, Oklahoma City would grow considerably in the postwar era, nearly a six-fold increase in its overall footprint by 1960. Once again, similar to several other U.S. cities, many retailers had left downtown Oklahoma City by the early '60s. City fathers decided that urban redevelopment was the answer and commissioned I. M. Pei to develop the plan. Pei advocated large-scale demolition of the central area, and in slightly more than a decade, it took shape—530 buildings were gone. Owing to large-scale abandonment of downtown by the retail stores, the hoped-for redevelopment did not materialize. Main no longer is a through street east of Hudson. Today, the Devon Energy Center Parking Garage stands in the street's former path.

B. L. Stone photo

23

MARION RAILWAYS NO. 12

Fourth and Adams, Marion, Indiana | August 12, 1946

Contraction of the Indiana interurban network led to the demise of several small-town streetcar operations as local power and repair facilities were no longer supported. Local interests in Marion were determined that this would not happen to that system. Following abandonment of the Frankfort-Marion-Anderson line by Indiana Railroad on July 1, 1932, Marion Railways Inc. was established to take over the streetcar operation.

Eventually amassing a fleet of 25 Birney cars, 18 of which had come from Union Traction, Marion Railways added to its wartime roster with cars built for Grand Rapids, St. Petersburg, and Springfield, Ill. Marion was unique in that it was the last all-Birney operation in the Midwest, with streetcar operations ending postwar, due to deteriorating condition of the physical plant. Typical of many Midwestern networks, the focal point of the streetcar system was the block bounding the 1882-vintage Grant County courthouse. Car 12 is shown at the southeast corner of that block, eastbound on Fourth at Adams.

B. L. Stone photo

25

City Lines of West Virginia No. 803

Market Street, Parkersburg, West Virginia | August 18, 1946

The 1928 10-car order from Kuhlman for Monongahela West Penn assigned the even-numbered cars to interurban service and the odds to city service. Monongahela West Penn was succeeded by City Lines of West Virginia (no relation to National City Lines) in 1943. Car 803 heads west on Market at Seventh in Parkersburg en route to the American Viscose Plant on August 18, 1946. More than half this line was on private right-of-way to approximately where it crossed the Baltimore & Ohio and the Kanawha River. The Viscose car line quit running on May 25, 1947. The B&O (which was then Parkersburg's third-largest employer) took over switching duties at the plant after the car line's abandonment. The plant, located southeast of the city, was the company's largest facility (33 acres under roof) and employed more than 4,000 people in the production of rayon yarn. American Viscose's operation was sold to FMC in 1963, and the Parkersburg Plant was closed in late 1974.

B. L. Stone photo

27

ATCHISON, TOPEKA & SANTA FE FT NO. 168L

Newton, Kansas | December 3, 1946

Santa Fe's Train 7, the *Fast Mail*, heads west through Newton, Kansas, on December 3, 1946. The trip from Chicago to Los Angeles required four 11-man Railway Post Office (RPO) crews. A typical consist included a working RPO and multiple mail storage cars. Three of the clerks were assigned exclusively to first class mail, another was responsible for newspapers, one handled registered mail, while another dealt with mixed mail. The balance of the mail clerks were assigned to sort mail for specific on-line states including Oklahoma, Texas, Colorado, New Mexico, Arizona, and California. Heading this day's train, Electro-Motive Division FT No. 168L had begun its Santa Fe career in May 1945. In the summer of 1946, it was converted to passenger service. Reconversion to freight duty occurred in December 1951. The locomotive was traded in to Electro-Motive in May 1962.

B. L. Stone photo

DALLAS RAILWAY & TERMINAL NO. 190

Market Street, Dallas, Texas | December 4, 1946

Stone & Webster took over the management of the Dallas streetcar system from 1902. Dallas-assigned cars with Stone & Webster's signature turtleback-roofed design came from three builders – American (a Brill subsidiary), Cincinnati, and St. Louis. Car 190 was part of a 10-car order delivered by St. Louis in 1913. The 102 cars of this design continued to serve successor company Dallas Railway & Terminal (adopted in 1926) and ran until late in the postwar conversion process with the last being retired in 1954. The last of the Dallas streetcar lines was converted to bus on January 15, 1956. The building to the right of the streetcar was Katy's headquarters in Dallas. A contemporary of streetcar 190, (construction was completed in 1914), the building has been renovated to provide new-gen office space. This area, just a few blocks southeast of Dealey Plaza, is part of Dallas's West End Historic District.

B. L. Stone photo

31

CHICAGO NORTH SHORE & MILWAUKEE NO. 500

Genesee Street, Waukegan, Illinois | 1947

North Shore's beginnings were in Waukegan as the Bluff City Electric, incorporated in September 1894. An 1895 extension to North Chicago built this section of line along Genesee Street. This part of the streetcar line was also used by interurbans operating to and from the County Street terminal. North Shore's franchise for Waukegan city operations expired in late 1947, not long after this view. Buses replaced the streetcars, including the 1909-vintage 500, one of five such St. Louis-built cars used along with Birneys and newer double-truck cars to provide service. The 500-series cars had been used on North Shore's Milwaukee city car operation until 1923. Sister car 509 was used as a waiting room at 10th Street station until being retired in 1948. The turreted and copper-clad building appearing above the 500 dated to the first year of Bluff City Electric. Condemned in 1986, the building stood unoccupied until finally being demolished in 2015.

W. C. Janssen photo

33

MEMPHIS STREET RAILWAY NO. 305

Union near Second, Memphis, Tennessee | circa 1947

Memphis Street Railway No. 305, part of the property's 1923 order from St. Louis Car, heads west on Union approaching Second Street in this 1947 view. Four streetcar lines had survived the war, but their operation would end this coming June 14th. As recently as 1942, the four lines had accounted for 32 percent of the company's gross revenues and 18 percent of net earnings.

All the buildings on the north side of Union have been replaced. A high-rise Holiday Inn has taken the place of the two-story structure immediately behind the streetcar. The classic five-story commercial building on the northwest corner of Union has been replaced by the multistory Commerce Square parking facility. To find a surviving structure from the prewar era, you must go down two blocks to Union and Main where the 14-story Farnsworth Building, dating to 1927, still stands. Named for C.F. Farnsworth, who financed the skyscraper, today the Memphis Heritage Streetcar runs north-south along the Main Street side of this building.

N. MacDonald photo

35

PERE MARQUETTE E7 NO. 102

Franklin Street, Grand Rapids, Michigan | circa 1947

Three months before D-Day, the Pere Marquette placed orders for its streamlined *Pere Marquette* trainsets. A pair of Electro-Motive Division E7s was also ordered and was completed in June 1946. The Pullman-built cars arrived two months later, and on August 10, 1946, the streamliners began Detroit-Grand Rapids service. Six additional E7s were received by the PM, four with April 1947 builder's dates and the final pair in August of that year.

While all this was taking place, the road's board of directors had approved a merger with the Chesapeake & Ohio on December 4, 1945. The merger agreement was executed the following February, and the ICC approved the merger on April 1, 1947. No. 102, part of that first order, leads Train 4 southbound at Franklin Street, Grand Rapids, circa 1947. The 102 remained on the C&O roster, later as the 4522 and then as the 1425, until being sold for scrap in 1968.

Krambles-Peterson Archive

MILWAUKEE ELECTRIC RAILWAY & LIGHT No. 863

Third near Michigan, Milwaukee, Wisconsin | July 16, 1947

Third and Michigan was once prime real estate in Milwaukee—just two blocks north of the Milwaukee Road depot, three blocks east of the North Shore Line terminal, and immediately in front of the Public Service Building where the Milwaukee Electric trains terminated. A wide variety of hotels and entertainment venues still greeted the traveler in July 1947. The Hotel Medford to the left of TM 863 dated to 1916. Right behind the streetcar was the Davidson Theater, which opened its doors in 1890. On the east side of Third, the marquee for the Violina Room and the associated Hotel Kilbourn catches your view. The Violina Room was so-named due to the many top violinists who played engagements there. The Davidson was demolished in 1954, followed by the Medford in 1964 and the Kilbourn in 1965. A parking lot, the Grand Avenue Mall, and a Marriott Courtyard Motel stand today where Third once ran.

T. H. Desnoyers photo

39

CINCINNATI, NEWPORT & COVINGTON NO. 511

Court Street, Covington, Kentucky | circa 1948

A southbound Belt Line car has come off Roebling Bridge, running down Court Street in Covington. The bridge, on which construction was begun in 1856 but not completed until 1867 due to a financial panic and the Civil War, dramatically changed Covington's fortunes. No longer would connection to Cincinnati be dependent on a ferry trying to thread the maze of dense river traffic on the Ohio. Horsecars from Covington (and later, Newport) used the suspension bridge. In the late 1890s, the bridge was extensively rebuilt, including a second set of main cables to allow electric streetcars to cross it. A further boost for the cross-river streetcars occurred in 1921 when they began to use the Dixie Terminal in downtown Cincinnati, avoiding on-street traffic delays. The last Green Line streetcars ran on July 2, 1950. Dual overhead in this view served the CN&C trolley-buses, which ran until March 17, 1958.

B. L. Stone photo

TEXAS ELECTRIC NO. 328

Hillsboro, Texas | July 3, 1948

Texas Electric experienced three serious accidents between 1946 and 1948, and in the wake of the Interstate Commerce Commission's recommendation that the entire system be signaled, the only sound economic move was to abandon service. The Central Electric Railfans' Association quickly organized a two-day trip on the road, with car 328 used on the Waco Line trip on July 3, 1948. The car is shown running northbound through Hillsboro next to the then-famous Grimes Garage. Unable to advertise in print or on the radio, the garage became famous for a series of 6-foot long 1 x 12 signs nailed to trees, wherever the law allowed them. Compensation for allowing a Grimes sign to be nailed to your tree was typically a silver dollar. The Grimes signs disappeared at the same time as Burma Shave signs went away, in the wake of a 1963 federal regulation.

B. L. Stone photo

43

WESTERN PACIFIC NO. 485

Second Street, Salt Lake City, Utah | July 7, 1948

Faced with wartime production restrictions, Western Pacific chose to piggyback on Southern Pacific's 1943 GS-6 order for 10 4-8-4 locomotives. Southern Pacific's nod to the restrictions was to reclassify the locomotives' GS classification as General Service (mixed freight and passenger duties); previously GS had meant Golden State class on the SP. Western Pacific's GS-64 order included six locomotives closely conforming to SP's specifications. SP-patented devices/designs were not used on the WP locomotives.

No. 485, shown on Second Street South in Salt Lake City on July 7, 1948, ran for just eight years, while other members of this WP class operated as late as 1953. The tender of WP 484 managed to survive as part of a supply train in rotary snowplow service and is at the Western Pacific Railroad Museum today. Southern Pacific's 4460 ran on several special trips commemorating the end of SP steam in October of 1958 and is preserved at the Museum of Transportation in St. Louis.

B. L. Stone photo

BIRMINGHAM ELECTRIC NO. 842

83rd and First, Birmingham, Alabama | circa 1949

The North Eastlake neighborhood is one of the oldest planned communities in Birmingham, having been established in 1886. By late 1887, the steam-hauled East Lake Railroad was in operation, with its barn less than a mile from the location of this photo, First Avenue North and 83rd Street North. The steam trains were replaced by electric cars, and in 1910, Birmingham annexed East Lake. The decade from 1940 to 1950 saw the Birmingham-area population swell by more than 20 percent. At the close of the war, Birmingham Electric rostered 27 distinct types of streetcars, some more than 40 years old. The company foresaw a decline in transit usage in the postwar era and ordered 48 PCCs to equip the four car lines it planned to retain. Fast acceleration and deceleration of the PCCs led to implementing express service on these lines. Here, No. 842 is working a West End Express not long after its delivery.

B. L. Stone photo

47

MEMPHIS UNION STATION SW1 NO. 10

Union Station, Memphis, Tennessee | circa 1949

Memphis Union Station SW1 No. 10 went to work in January 1942. In this 1949 view near the west side of Union Station, the office building for Central Station can been seen off to the left of the locomotive. When the Missouri Pacific ceased to use Union Station, that left only Louisville & Nashville and Southern Railway in that facility. These roads were unwilling to bear the cost of operating and maintaining Union Station. On the station's closing in 1964, the locomotive went to work for Republic Steel. After 20 years at a Thomas, Alabama, plant, it is now part of the Heart of Dixie Museum's collection.

As it happens, the city of Memphis forced the reopening of Union Station in December 1966. However, as the remaining tenants, L&N and Southern agreed that no switching work would be done in the revived station. Union Station's second closing was effective March 30, 1968. The property was sold and the Beaux-Arts terminal building was demolished.

B. L. Stone photo

49

MILWAUKEE ROAD NO. 152

Milwaukee, Wisconsin | June 4, 1949

Milwaukee's Gothic-styled Everett Street Station offers an amazing array of train action on the early afternoon of June 4, 1949. From left, there's the nose of Milwaukee Road Atlantic No. 3, barely visible behind an SW1 waiting to handle station switching chores, Fairbanks-Morse Erie-A 12B on the west-bound *Afternoon Hiawatha*, and F3as 152 waiting on the *Hiawatha's* departure to get its *Chippewa Hiawatha* underway. Beyond the baggage cars farther to the right, the tail end of the *Afternoon Hiawatha* wraps around. Given that the star of this show is the *Afternoon Hi*, it's likely the 152 is in the process of backing out of its way. The No. 3, ready to handle the *North Woods Hiawatha*, may well be sitting uncoupled, to not block passenger access to the *Afternoon Hi*. The Atlantic would be pulled out of service in just three months' time to become a parts source for its sister engines.

H. M. Stange photo

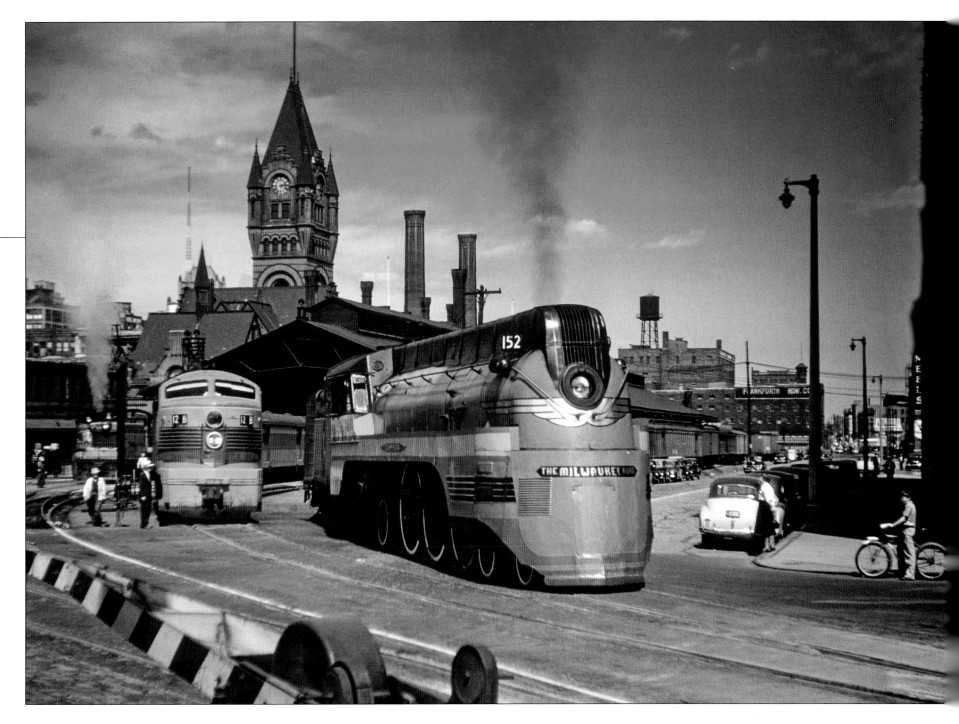

PACIFIC ELECTRIC NO. 1120

Fair Oaks and Green, Pasadena, California | September 11, 1949

Pacific Electric's 50-car order for 1100-series suburban cars was delivered from Standard Steel Car in the second half of 1924. Thereafter, these cars were fixtures on the Pasadena lines, both those routed via Oak Knoll and those using the Short Line. The Short Line was about 2.5 miles shorter and saved around 10 to 15 minutes versus the Oak Knoll trips.

The New Year's Tournament of Roses Parade saw ridership to and from Pasadena explode. Three-car trains were required to handle the crowds, and cars from other PE districts were brought in to supplement the 1100s. On a more typical day in Pasadena, car 1120 is shown southbound on Fair Oaks at Green on September 11, 1949. This car was withdrawn from service following accident damage that occurred on May 11, 1950. It was repaired by PE's Torrance Shops prior to sale of the entire class for continued use in Buenos Aires in 1952.

H. M. Stange photo

RIO GRANDE SOUTHERN NO. 5

Seventh Street, Dolores, Colorado | September 11, 1949

Rio Grande Southern motor 5 is eastbound at Seventh Street in Dolores, Colorado, on September 11, 1949. The seven motorcars, nicknamed the Galloping Geese, were built by RGS's Ridgway Shops as a means of reducing operating costs. In the case of the 5, it was built in 1933 using parts from a 1928 Pierce-Arrow auto. This originally included a Pierce Series 36, dual-valve, six-cylinder engine. Completion of motor 5 allowed the RGS to replace all regular steam-powered passenger service. Postwar, RGS re-bodied No. 5 with a Wayne bus body, and a GMC engine replaced the Pierce-Arrow motor in 1947. Cancellation of RGS's post office contract (due to unreliability) in March 1950 led to RGS putting No. 5 (among other motors) into tourist service. The last tourist trips ran in October 1951, and the last freight ran to Dolores on December 29, 1951. Abandonment permission was granted on April 24, 1952.

B. L. Stone photo

Key System No. 139

Claremont Hotel, Berkeley, California | September 14, 1949

Francis "Borax" Smith and his partners invested their fortunes in 13,000 undeveloped East Bay-area acres in October 1903 and opened the rail service that would famously become the Key System to stimulate growth. The fast, frequent electric trains had the desired impact. They also forced competitor Southern Pacific to up its game and electrify its East Bay suburban services. Smith and partners invested in two hotels to further stimulate Key Route patronage. An eponymously named hotel (later destroyed by fire) opened in 1907, while the Claremont Hotel at the end of the Key E line opened in 1915. The main building of the Claremont is in Oakland, while the spa, gardens, and parking area are in Berkeley. For a fan, the attraction was that simple, direct connection the stylish "bridge units" provided by slipping between the hotel's tennis courts.

H. M. Stange photo

SAN FRANCISCO MUNICIPAL RAILWAY NO. 1002

Market and Eddy, San Francisco, California | September 15, 1949

The Municipal Railway bought five "Magic Carpet" streamliners from St. Louis Car in 1939 for $22,000 each. Three of the cars (including the 1002 shown westbound on Market at Eddy on September 15, 1949) rode on Clark B-2 trucks, while the other pair was delivered with Brill 97ER1 trucks. Of this group, only No. 1003 was preserved; the other four cars went for scrap in 1959.

The Flood Building, behind the car, dated to 1904 and was one of the few downtown buildings to survive the 7.8-magnitude earthquake of April 18, 1906. The quake ruptured gas mains, leading to numerous fires, which burned for several days and destroyed almost 25,000 buildings in the city. The Southern Pacific was later a tenant in the Flood Building, prior to moving to Market Street in 1917. This section of Market once hosted the famous four tracks used by cars of both the Muni and Market Street Railway.

H. M. Stange photo

PORTLAND TRACTION CO. NO. 509

Burnside and 19th, Portland, Oregon | September 16, 1949

Portland Traction had cut back the Council Crest line over the final half-mile to a terminal at Patton and Vista just the month before this September 1949 view at northwest 19th and Burnside. No. 509 was one of 10 cars bought from Brill in 1904 for ultimate use on the Council Crest line, which went into service on September 20, 1906. The streetcar company built an amusement park at the peak, which remained in operation until 1929. The land was acquired by the city in 1937, but the removal of the amusement park buildings wasn't completed until 1941. Final abandonment of the truncated Council Crest route occurred on February 26, 1950, when the Willamette Heights and 23rd Avenue carlines were also converted to bus, closing out streetcar service. Sister car 506 was preserved at Council Crest from 1950 until 1972. Today, successor Tri-Met's MAX light rail line runs about two blocks south of this location.

H. M. Stange photo

61

INDIANAPOLIS RAILWAYS NO. 136

Fairfield-College, Indianapolis, Indiana | circa 1950

In a period of grave economic concern, Indianapolis Railways took a tremendous chance ordering 90 new streetcars from Brill in 1932 and 1934. Incorporating General Electric's PCM control equipment and foot pedals at the operator's station, with elements of the Brill "Master Unit" design, these cars would operate in Indianapolis until the end of streetcar service in January 1953. Working the Illinois line, car 136 (from the 1934 order) is eastbound on Fairfield at College circa 1950. College Avenue had also been the route that Indiana Railroad interurban trains to/from Peru and Kokomo used to enter and leave Indianapolis until September 1938. The row of stores is an empty lot today. To identify this scene, it was necessary to locate the peaked-roof apartment building in the distant background at the left edge of the photo.

W. B. Cox photo

63

CINCINNATI STREET RAILWAY NO. 1355

Spring Grove Avenue, Cincinnati, Ohio | March 5, 1950

Construction of Cincinnati's Western Hills Viaduct between 1930 and 1932 improved streetcar service to the Fairmount and Westwood Hills area, but also aided auto access as well, sowing the seeds of the transit system's demise. At its east end, the viaduct spanned Spring Grove Avenue and provided this vantage point for a snapshot of the Cincinnati Street Railway in transition. A 1948 Marmon-Herrington trolleybus working the 31-Crosstown line is followed by a 1923-vintage Cincinnati-built "curved-side" car on route 18-North Fairmount. Both these vehicles will use the lower deck of the viaduct; this view also shows how the unique double-overhead used by the streetcars facilitated trolleybus conversion. For example, the 31 line had been converted for trolleybuses on April 11, 1948. The substation and factory building on the west side of Spring Grove Avenue still stand. Everything to the east of the avenue was wiped out by the early 1960s construction of I-75.

Krambles-Peterson Archive

SCRANTON TRANSIT NO. 419

Cedar Avenue, Scranton, Pennsylvania | June 30, 1950

George W. and Selden T. Scranton established a predecessor of Lackawanna Steel in the 1840s. The brothers were also instrumental in the building of the Lackawanna & Western Railroad in 1851, which was absorbed into the Delaware, Lackawanna & Western around 1856. For the next century, the DL&W would be the top employer in Scranton. The shops complex in the Keyser Valley dated to the early part of the 20th century and was finally closed in the mid-1960s. The decorative DL&W concrete fence post just to the left of Scranton Transit car 419 still stands today, as does the tower seen at the right above the car at the Lackawanna station. The DL&W track crossing Cedar Avenue remains in place and is used by the Electric City Trolley Museum. Scranton's last streetcar (to Green Ridge) quit running December 18, 1954.

H. M. Stange photo

VIRGINIAN NO. 103

Covel, West Virginia | June 28, 1950

The Virginian's 1925 electrification of the Mullens-Roanoke line was intended to tame the stiff grades that loaded coal trains encountered between Elmore and Algonquin, as well as to nearly double the tonnage per train. Design criteria for the three-unit electrics also called for an increase in train speeds from 7 mph to 14 mph. The 7,100 hp units could produce a starting tractive effort of 277,500 pounds. One of the most famous locations on the electrified zone was the trestle over Gooney Otter Creek and the road leading east into the hollow. No. 103 leads a train past Covel (not a stop on the Virginian) on June 28, 1950. Covel is halfway between Micahjah (MP 364) and Herndon (MP 368). Speed limit on the trestle was 25 mph. Surviving into the Norfolk & Western merger, the electrics on the former Virginian line last operated on June 30, 1962.

H. M. Stange photo

69

PHILADELPHIA SUBURBAN TRANSPORTATION NO. 85

West Chester Pike near Darby Road, Upper Darby, Pennsylvania | September 1950

Philadelphia & West Chester Traction began electric car service on West Chester Pike on January 4, 1899. A branch to Ardmore joined the West Chester line near Darby Road and is the location of this September 1950 photo. Electric cars to Ardmore began operation on May 29, 1902. Philadelphia & West Chester Traction also established its Llanerch Car House just past the Darby Road junction. The Brills, including No. 85 depicted here, were P&WCT's first one-man cars and were delivered in 1932. The operation was reorganized as Philadelphia Suburban Transportation in 1936. With the postwar increase in automobile registrations, a project to widen West Chester Pike was begun in the early 1950s, with rail service being an immediate victim. West Chester cars were cut back to West Gate Hills in 1954 and abandoned altogether in August 1958. The last cars to Ardmore ran in late December 1966.

G. Krambles photo

ANACONDA STREET RAILWAY NO. 16

Anaconda, Montana | September 4, 1950

Outside of shift changes at the copper smelter, operations on the Anaconda Street Railway took on a relaxed air, such as car 16 heading east on Third at Main on September 4, 1950. Five-car motor-trailer trains were not uncommon in the peak. A provision of the smelter employees' labor contract stipulated that they had reported to work once they were on the train. The building behind the car once housed the *Anaconda Standard*, as well as the offices of the town's electric light company. The paper, just as the town, the trolley, and the smelter, owed their existence to Marcus Daly, who established the smelter in 1883. Buses replaced the electric cars on the last day of 1951, while the smelter shut down in 1980. Today, the building serves as the local Elks Lodge, and the church a block down has also continued in use.

H. M. Stange photo

73

British Columbia Electric No. 124

Victory Square, Vancouver, British Columbia | September 7, 1950

British Columbia Electric Railway observation car 124 (home-built in 1909) takes its layover at Vancouver's Victory Square in September 1950. Although the peak ridership for BCER's observation cars had been in 1947 (when 35,000 used the service), ongoing conversion of the streetcar system to bus/trolleybus reduced the available track miles such that a practical sightseeing route was no longer feasible. The advertising sign on the front of the car already reflects a drastic reduction of this service, which would make its last run 10 days later on September 17, 1950. The last of Vancouver's streetcars would operate on the Hastings East Line on April 24, 1955.

The building looming over the 124 on the corner of Cambie and Hastings is the 1898-vintage Flack Block, built by Thomas Flack, an early Klondike prospector. The building survives, thoroughly cleaned-up and magnificently restored. To the right of the sightseeing car is the former *Vancouver Province* building, dating to 1908.

H. M. Stange photo

CEDAR RAPIDS & IOWA CITY NO. 119

Second Street Wye, Cedar Rapids, Iowa | 1951

Modernization of CRANDIC's passenger fleet was accomplished by purchasing six ex-Cincinnati & Lake Erie Red Devil lightweights in 1939 and a single ex-Indiana Railroad Highspeed in 1941. The single-end cars were wyed at Second Street and Fourth Avenue in Cedar Rapids, as the 119 is doing in this 1951 view. The background is dominated by Killian's Department Store, which opened in 1911 and originated the use of the "door-buster" sale around 1917. Today, this building is the headquarters of an architectural engineering firm. Across the street, the Paramount theater's marquee stands out. Opened in 1928 as the Capitol, the theater was sold and had been renamed by 1929. Restoration work has been undertaken on this facility three times, most recently after a disastrous 2008 flood. Farther north on Second Street is the 12-story Roosevelt Hotel, which opened in 1927. Finally, at the far north end of the street is the Quaker Oats Cereal Mill, built in 1926–27 and hailed as the "world's largest cereal factory."

W. C. Janssen photo

FORT DODGE, DES MOINES & SOUTHERN NO. 72

Story Street, Boone, Iowa | May 6, 1951

In 1951, when Fort Dodge, Des Moines & Southern's car 72 paused at the Boone depot, the railway posted total revenues of $2.3 million and net earnings of $208,000. As you'd expect, this was largely on the strength of the 31,000 freight cars the line had handled that year, and of these, more than half carried gypsum products. Significant gypsum and other mineral deposits were located in the Fort Dodge area, and their proximity to the rich farming area led to an increase in the use of the mineral on farms. Gypsum has also been used for thousands of years as a building material, from the Egyptian pyramids to today's wallboard, cement, and plaster of paris. In the wake of flood damage at FDDM&S's Fraser power plant, the line was de-electrified in 1955. Passenger service also ended at this time. Under Chicago & North Western ownership from 1968, the Boone station was demolished in 1973.

B. L. Stone photo

ILLINOIS TRACTION NO. 263

Vermillion Street, Danville, Illinois | June 10, 1951

William B. McKinley's Illinois Traction empire had its beginnings in Danville with the purchase of the city's streetcar system in 1901. The following year, the line was extended west to Urbana. Five decades later, car 263 (a 1911 product of the hometown carbuilder) waits on its 11:05 a.m. departure time as Train 63. No. 263 will cover nearly all the 80-odd miles to Decatur before it is scheduled to meet another train, eastbound Train 62 at Leslie (near Cerro Gordo). From Decatur, it will continue another 37 miles to Springfield, meeting Train 64 at Starnes on the north side of town, where the Illinois Central and Wabash were crossed at-grade. Train 63 was scheduled to cover the 120 miles in 3 hours, 40 minutes, averaging 32.3 mph. The IT stopped serving Danville on April 27, 1952, when the line was cut back to Ogden. No. 263 was one of three cars modified with a front pole to allow it to wye in Ogden.

H. M. Stange photo

Milwaukee Rapid Transit & Speedrail No. 60

Madison and Clinton, Waukesha, Wisconsin | June 10, 1951

Speedrail was in the last month of its brief existence when Henry Stange shot eastbound car 60 in front of the Waukesha interurban station in early June 1951. A Waukesha Transit Line Ford bus is visible two blocks behind the curved-sider. The accidents that plagued Speedrail in February and September 1950 put the line into an insurance crisis that might have forced its shutdown even sooner, had there not been a last-minute reprieve in the form of a new insurance plan.

The six Cincinnati-built cars had an amazing resume, especially considering how late they had come along in the life of interurbans. In the case of No. 60, it was built as Indianapolis & South Eastern's car 260 in 1929. On cessation of I&SE's operations in 1932, it was returned to the car builder. In 1935, Inter-City Rapid Transit acquired the car and ran it as car 260 for the next seven years. At that point, it became Cleveland Interurban Railway No. 60, transitioning to Shaker Heights Rapid Transit ownership from 1944. Replaced by PCCs on the Shaker, it was sold to E.L. Tennyson in 1949 and leased to Speedrail.

H. M. Stange photo

CHICAGO & ILLINOIS MIDLAND NO. 547

Springfield, Illinois | August 19, 1951

During the government administration of U.S. railroads, 175 United States Railroad Administration standard design 0-8-0 locomotives were built. However, in the period following the dissolution of the USRA (in 1920), another 1,200 locomotives were built to this design. Chicago & Illinois Midland is an example of a post-USRA build. Built by Lima in 1926 as Kentucky & Indiana Terminal 27, it was sold to the C&IM in 1949. In December 1955, the 547 was retired and sold the following February to Old Sydney Colleries, becoming its No. 33. In this August 19, 1951, photo, the 547 is shown switching at the south (Phillips Street) end of the Springfield Yard with one of C&IM's 50-ton, outside-braced gondolas in tow. The background is dominated by the Pillsbury Mill, which, when opened in 1929, was one of the first non-coal industries on the C&IM. Demolition of the mill began in 2014, but was suspended due to improper handling of asbestos.

H. M. Stange photo

DELAWARE, LACKAWANNA & WESTERN NO. 814

Scranton, Pennsylvania | September 8, 1951

Dieselization of Lackawanna's passenger service began with five A-B-A sets of Electro-Motive Division F3s delivered in late 1946 and 1947. These bumped the Alco 1937-built 4-6-4s, as well as the 1927–1934 vintage 4-8-4 "Poconos," from key trains. Delivery of 11 E8s during 1951 largely finished the process. The Lackawanna received 10 steam generator-equipped Train Masters in 1953.

Lackawanna's E8 fleet included two ex-EMD demonstrators plus nine production units, a group that included the 814, shown here with Train 2, the *Pocono Express*, leaving Scranton. The vantage point is the Harrison Avenue viaduct, which spanned Roaring Brook and the Lackawanna & Wyoming Valley interurban line in addition to the DL&W. Later, the L&WV right-of-way would become the route for the Central Scranton Expressway. As for the 814, it survived into the merged Erie-Lackawanna fleet and made it to Conrail, which traded it in to EMD in May of 1977.

H. M. Stange photo

LEHIGH VALLEY TRANSIT NO. 419

Sixth and Gordon, Allentown, Pennsylvania | November 11, 1951

Sixth and Gordon in Allentown turns out to be one of the least-changed streetscapes included in this book. While paint color, siding, and roofing materials (along with building uses) may have changed, virtually every structure has survived to the current day. Benioff's [furriers] sign off to the left advertises the store at 410-414 N. Sixth, which had housed the firm since 1922. Workshops and vaults remained here after a new downtown location at 10th and Hamilton opened. Lehigh Valley Transit 419 was a 1923 Kuhlman-built car originally owned by the Ohio Valley Electric. All 14 cars from this order came to LVT in 1938 as part of a substantial modernization program for the Allentown-Bethlehem-Easton services. Cars built for the Jamestown Street Railway, the Williamsport Passenger Railway, and Wisconsin Public Service were among those LVT acquired in the late 1930s.

C. Houser photo

METROPOLITAN TRANSIT AUTHORITY 3270-CLASS

Causeway Elevated, Boston, Massachusetts | 1952

Credit Henry Stange for this superb look at Boston's beloved West End, just prior to the start of the area's redevelopment. The vantage point is the Manger Hotel, immediately west of Boston Garden and North Station. The Boston & Maine would later buy the Manger, by then renamed the Madison. The hotel closed in 1976 and was demolished in the 1980s. The Causeway Elevated had been in service for 40 years when Henry made this shot of an inbound train of MTA 3270-class PCC cars in 1952. Redevelopment of the West End was announced the following April. The 46-acre area was leveled, resulting in the displacement of nearly 3,000 families. The neighborhood's 1950 population had been nearly 12,000, and by 1970, it was less than 3,500. The Causeway Elevated continued in service until June 2004. MBTA's replacement subway opened for service in November 2005.

H. M. Stange photo

SEABOARD AIR LINE E7 NO. 3036

St. Petersburg, Florida | March 1952

The Seaboard station serving St. Petersburg in the early '50s was on the northwest corner of Ninth Street South and Second Avenue South. It dated to 1910 and had been built by the Tampa & Gulf Coast. A section of the *Silver Meteor* operated from Wildwood to Tampa/St. Petersburg, while the rest of the train headed to Miami. In Tampa, the train was again split into sections that would operate to Venice or to St. Petersburg. The *Meteor* also provided the connections for the *Tidewater* from Norfolk/Portsmouth and the *Gulf Wind* from New Orleans and other Gulf Coast locations. Successor Seaboard Coast Line would later discontinue the St. Petersburg section. It was revived under Amtrak, although operation was again cut back to Tampa on January 31, 1984. SAL E7 3036 was one of 32 units the road once rostered and is shown on in-street trackage in March 1952.

W. B. Cox photo

Chicago Aurora & Elgin No. 321

Marshfield Avenue, Chicago, Illinois | April 1952

The Chicago Aurora & Elgin was a significant west suburban transportation artery in the early 1950s. Morning rush service included 6 five-car trains, 6 sixes (including this westbound train shown at CA&E's dedicated Marshfield Avenue station in April 1952), 2 seven-car trains and 1 eight-car consist. A predecessor of the CA&E had been the first of the interurban companies to reach agreement to use an L line (in this case, the Metropolitan West Side Elevated Railroad) to reach downtown, with this agreement taking effect in March 1905. However, CA&E would cease to directly service downtown Chicago after September 20, 1953, when the Garfield Park L trains were re-routed to an at-grade alignment along Van Buren Street. This was done to facilitate construction of the Congress Street Expressway, which necessitated removal of the L and the surrounding buildings in this view.

G. Krambles photo

PITTSBURGH RAILWAYS CO. NO. 4394

Fifth Avenue, McKeesport, Pennsylvania | May 1952

The Glassport-Evans shuttle car has just a few more blocks to go before reaching its east terminal at Fifth and Evans in McKeesport. With no turning loops at either end, double-end cars like the 4394 were required. In this May 1952 view, it is crossing Baltimore & Ohio tracks adjacent to the road's McKeesport station. This grade crossing and the one across Lysle Boulevard (a block to the north) were real headaches to city fathers. A 1940 study had shown this crossing to be blocked for about four hours every day. In addition to Pittsburgh Railways' cars, 2,800 vehicles and 70,000 pedestrians crossed these tracks daily. As recently as 1948 McKeesport's downtown was generating $77 million in retail sales. Several proposals to address the grade crossing issues were floated. Rerouting of B&O trains onto Pittsburgh & Lake Erie tracks, which was the simplest alternative, was finally adopted.

R. V. Mehlenbeck photo

WEST PENN NO. 736

Pennsylvania and Second, Greensburg, Pennsylvania | May 30, 1952

For many electric railways, the Public Utilities Holding Act of 1935 was their death knell, requiring separation from the owning power companies. This was not the case for West Penn Railways, which from its 1917 reorganization had owned all of West Penn Power's stock. Over time, the extent of the railway's holding decreased, as the railway did not avail itself of the opportunity to buy newly issued power company shares, etc. World War II intervened, and the increased ridership helped to prolong the railway's financial viability. Still, by 1944, the railway prepared a policy statement (adopted in 1946) calling for abandonment of railway operation. Car 736, part of West Penn's 1924 build of center-door cars, is just a few blocks from the Greensburg terminal on May 30, 1952. Service between Irwin and Greensburg would end on July 12, 1952, while the Greensburg-Uniontown main line continued to run until August 9, 1952.

W. C. Janssen photo

PACIFIC GREAT EASTERN 70-TONNER NO. 556

Williams Lake, British Columbia | July 5, 1952

The challenging terrain in British Columbia forced the Pacific Great Eastern to build north from Squamish, rather than start from North Vancouver. It would not close the gap into North Vancouver until 1956. Pacific Great Eastern construction over the 275 miles to Williams Lake was completed in 1919, by which time the railroad had been acquired by the provincial government. Williams Lake (shown here) was PGE's northern railhead until 1921, when construction toward Quesnel was resumed. North of Quesnel, geography again challenged the road, and the line to Prince George was not completed until 1952.

Coincidentally, this photo of General Electric 70-tonner 556 on a work train was taken in 1952. The occasion was the operation of a "PGE Boosters" train on July 5. The 556 remained on the PGE roster until 1965, when it was sold to Lake Ontario Steel. Williams Lake began holding its Stampede in celebration of the railroad's arrival and has continued to do so to this day.

N. MacDonald photo

CHICAGO TRANSIT AUTHORITY NO. 248

63rd and Peoria, Chicago, Illinois | 1953

Pre-mall and before the big-box store era, there were several thriving commercial concentrations outside Chicago's Loop. One such area remembered with special fondness was Englewood's 63rd & Halsted shopping area. Chicago Transit Authority "Big Pullman" 248 is westbound on 63rd approaching Peoria, having passed the Art Deco Sears store at Halsted (where the Yusay Beer truck is crossing in the background). This was the era when People's Gas and Commonwealth Edison still had neighborhood branch stores for paying bills, buying light bulbs or appliances, and the like. It was also a period when neighborhood taverns still proliferated. During the immediate postwar era, there were almost 7,000 such establishments in Chicago. The two Mayors Daley both led drives to reduce the number of taverns, more than halving the total by 1989 and reducing it again by more than 60 percent in 2005, when just 1,300 such businesses were located within the city limits.

R. V. Mehlenbeck photo

CHICAGO, BURLINGTON & QUINCY E7 NO. 9919A

Omaha, Nebraska | circa 1953

Union Pacific broke ground in Omaha in late 1863, began rail-laying two years later in the city, and had built west across Nebraska by 1867. The Burlington & Missouri River had reached Omaha and opened its line to Lincoln by July 1870. Owing to excellent railroad connections such as these, the South Omaha Union Stockyards opened in 1883. Not long after this 1953 view, those stockyards surpassed the Chicago Union Stockyards. By 1957, the Omaha Stockyards and industries related to them accounted for the employment of half of Omaha's workforce. Competition for passengers was still intense in this pre-jet era. The UP ran seven daily round trips to/from Chicago via the C&NW connection, while the Burlington provided six daily round trips. The CB&Q offered the fastest timings, down to 7 hours, 30 minutes, though the UP-C&NW routing was highly competitive with some trains taking just 7 hours, 45 minutes to make the trip.

Krambles-Peterson Archive

TWIN CITY RAPID TRANSIT NO. 1833

Kellogg and Smith, St. Paul, Minnesota | circa 1953

Twin City Rapid Transit's Snelling Shops built 1,234 cars of the "standard" design, of which 1,128 were for use on TCRT's own routes. Car 1833, shown southbound on Kellogg at Smith in St. Paul circa 1953, was part of a 40-car order completed in 1917. These same shops converted the car to one-man operation in 1932. The car is working the Selby-Lake line, which would be converted to bus operation on July 10, 1953.

Thanks to the construction of I-35E (which opened to Kellogg Boulevard in 1988), and its complex junction with I-94 (which opened north of Kellogg in 1990), along with the 1998–2000 construction of the Xcel Energy Center event venue, this area is virtually unrecognizable. All the buildings in the background are gone, and of the businesses represented, only Schneider Flooring (the vertical sign above the refrigerated truck) remains in St. Paul, currently doing business at Seventh and Bay Streets.

J. R. Williams photo

CHICAGO TRANSIT AUTHORITY NO. 7040

Cottage Grove near 31st, Chicago, Illinois | March 3, 1953

What we lost: While your eyes are immediately drawn to those great arched bay windows and all the other architectural flourishes in the buildings to the left of the streetcar, this part of the near South Side (near 31st Street) had been down on its luck for a good while. Postwar surveys of the area indicated nearly 50 percent of residences in some blocks were dilapidated, while others still lacked electricity or indoor plumbing in 1949. Michael Reese Hospital (a few blocks north of this location), Illinois Institute of Technology, and Mercy Hospital jointly formed the South Side Planning Board in 1946 to address the needs of these declining neighborhoods. The following year, the state passed a Blighted Areas Redevelopment and Relocation Act to assist the process of clearing blighted areas. Ultimately, New York Life financed the Lake Meadows development, which unrecognizably transformed this neighborhood.

G. Krambles photo

NEW YORK CITY TRANSIT AUTHORITY LO-V TRAIN

Broadway and 122nd, New York, New York | December 1953

The Manhattanville neighborhood centers on Broadway and 125th Street in New York. When the original Interborough Rapid Transit subway was being designed, a separate construction contract was issued for the 0.4-mile-long Manhattan Valley viaduct, extending between 122nd and 135th Streets, where it tied in to the subways. This avoided having sharp changes in grade, which would have been required had the line remained in a subway across the valley. In addition, it also avoided a fault line running under 125th Street. Service on the West Side Line began on October 27, 1904. A typical midday train made up of Lo-V cars heads into the subway at 122nd Street in December 1953. Interborough Rapid Transit bought nearly 1,400 of these cars from four builders (including conversions of cars performed in its own shops) between 1915 and 1942. Last operation of the Lo-Vs (so named for the use of low-voltage control circuits) on this line occurred in February 1959.

J. W. Vigrass photo

CHICAGO & NORTH WESTERN F7 NO. 4085A

De Kalb, Illinois | 1954

North Western predecessor Galena & Chicago Union reached De Kalb in August 1853, when there were all of 29 residents in the town. Double-tracking of the rail line through here was completed in 1891. A quantum leap in capacity of the rail line was achieved in the late 1920s when new GRS signals replaced a mixture of Hall signals and semaphores on the Geneva Subdivision. The new signals included a third aspect, as well as longer blocks. Within a year or two, the Class H Northerns arrived, boosting tonnage per train by nearly 50 percent. Centralized Traffic Control was installed on this line between West Chicago and Nelson (46 miles west of De Kalb) in 1950. Additional capacity improvements occurred with each model of road freight diesel. For example, a two-unit F7 (such as this A-B team) was rated for 12 percent greater tonnage than a Class H. The train is eastbound crossing the Lincoln Highway in 1954.

H. M. Stange photo

CLEVELAND TRANSIT SYSTEM NO. 4105

Bridge and 65th, Cleveland, Ohio | 1954

The Madison-Lakewood route was Cleveland's last streetcar line, converted to buses on January 23, 1954. Not long before the end, car 4105 (a 1930 Kuhlman) prepares to swing through the intersection of Bridge and 65th. From this location, the cars ran one-quarter mile south on Bridge to Madison and then an additional 4½ miles west to a wye at Spring Garden Avenue. Thirty of the 100 cars from this order were retained to run this route. Normally operated from the West 117th Street Barn, which fronted on the Madison section of this line, a gas explosion on West 117th isolated the cars from that barn, necessitating wire to be strung to allow the cars to reach the Denison Barn at Denison and 73rd. The turreted apartment house behind the car still stands while neighborhood stores stand on the other corners of this intersection. Greater Cleveland Regional Transit Authority route 45/45A runs from Bridge Avenue onto West 65th Street.

J. W. Vigrass photo

East Broad Top No. 18

Robertsdale, Pennsylvania | 1954

East Broad Top in the 1950s was a string of lasts—mail runs ended after 80 years of service in 1953, the last passenger trains operated in August 1954, and finally the entire rail operation closed in April 1956. Coal demand (90 percent of EBT's postwar revenue stream) had dropped sharply, including the shift of area industries (brick plants, etc.) to oil and gas, making the railroad redundant. Rescue of the road by the Kovalchick family and the preservation of the company town of Robertsdale is well known in railfan circles. Mikado No. 18 is shown in Robertsdale in 1954. Part of a three-locomotive order from Baldwin in 1916, these locomotives increased total locomotive weight by 6 percent compared to their 1912 predecessors. Thanks to an increase in combined heating surface area with significant superheating, as well as larger, high-pressure cylinders, the last three Mikes increased tractive effort by 11 percent to 30,600 pounds. Nos. 16 and 18 have remained in storage since EBT's 1956 shutdown.

B. L. Stone photo

GREATER WINNIPEG TRANSIT COMMISSION NO. 712

Portage and Duff, Winnipeg, Manitoba | circa 1954

Winnipeg's first horsecars ran in October 1882. A trial of electric streetcars started in January 1891, with regular operation of the new technology beginning in September 1892. Streetcar service on this section of Portage Avenue (west-southwest of downtown) began circa 1903. The car depicted, No. 712, is part of the 1919 order of Ottawa-built cars the Winnipeg Electric Company received. By the time of this 1954 photo, management responsibility had been assumed by the Greater Winnipeg Transit Commission. In 1954, the Portage-North Main route still required 80 cars for peak period service. The GWTC would oversee the transition to an all-bus operation in September 1955. The buildings to the left of the streetcar are the Deer Lodge Hospital, opened in 1916 as a military convalescent facility. Transitioning to provincial ownership in 1983, the Deer Lodge Centre remains in operation today as a long-term care and rehabilitation facility.

N. MacDonald photo

ILLINOIS CENTRAL NO. 1237

Baton Rouge, Louisiana | circa 1954

At 455.9 miles, the Yazoo & Mississippi Valley Memphis-New Orleans line was 62 miles longer than Illinois Central's line between the two cities. Merged into the IC in 1946, the Y&MV had delivered the construction materials for the Louisiana State Capitol, towering above the first gondola behind the engine in this 1954 view. With a height of 450 feet, Louisiana's capitol was the tallest in the United States when it opened in mid-1932.

The Mikado is drawing alongside the Y&MV depot, which today is the Art & Science Museum in Baton Rouge. The Lima-built Mike was delivered to the IC as its 1739 in 1915. Renumbered in October 1942, the locomotive was one of 37 Mikes assigned to IC's Vicksburg Division in 1953. Even at that late date, the group of 2-8-2s constituted nearly half of all the locomotives assigned to that division. No. 1237 was retired and scrapped in 1955.

J. Schmidt photo

Johnstown Traction Co. No. 405

Main near Market Street, Johnstown, Pennsylvania | circa 1954

There were no license plates visible to date this view, but the "Penn Traffic 100th Year" sign on the mountain pins this down as 1954. Penn Traffic was founded in the same year the Pennsylvania Railroad reached Johnstown, 1854. The famous store would file for bankruptcy in late 2009. Other western Pennsylvania institutions have located their advertising signs in clear view of downtown workers and shoppers. Duquesne Pilsener began brewing in 1899 and closed its doors in 1972. In the case of Fort Pitt Beer, it stopped brewing in 1957 after 51 years in the business. Both brews have recently been revived.

Of the buildings in the block where PCC 405 is running (westbound on Main near Market), the Penney's building is gone, as is the camera store. Successor transit operator Cam Trans has an off-street bus terminal at that location. The buildings occupied by Household Finance and Triangle Shoes are still standing, as is the building that then accommodated Kinney Shoes—the 1883-vintage Stenger Store.

B. L. Stone photo

KANSAS CITY PUBLIC SERVICE NO. 769

St. Louis Avenue Station, Kansas City, Missouri | July 2, 1954

A unified stockyard was established in the Kansas City West Bottoms area/Central Industrial District from 1871. Ten separate rail carriers were serving West Bottoms by 1880, and in 1888, the Eighth Street Tunnel (through Quality Hill) and the elevated line extending west from the tunnel had been opened by the grandly named Interstate Consolidated Rapid Transit Company. Originally used by cable cars, the tunnel and elevated structure were converted for electric car operation in 1892. In 1904, the 8 percent grade in the tunnel was reduced and the tunnel was extended east to Broadway. The 1951 flood, which saw 2 million acres underwater, is felt to have dealt the stockyards an unrecoverable blow. Kansas City Public Service PCC 769 is shown at the St. Louis Avenue elevated station on July 2, 1954. The tracks in the shadow of the elevated streetcar structure are those of the Missouri Pacific. To the left of the view is the Wabash freight station (at 1010 St. Louis Avenue).

J. W. Vigrass photo

RUTLAND RS3 NO. 206

Harbor Road, Shelburne, Vermont | September 5, 1954

The Rutland Railway emerged from receivership on November 1, 1950. Over the next two years, the road dieselized with a single GE 70-tonner, six Alco RS1s and nine RS3s. In late June 1953, operating employees struck the Rutland for three weeks; the road's passenger service was then eliminated. This photo of two RS3s making time with the World of Mirth show train was taken September 5, 1954. The train is southbound crossing Harbor Road in Shelburne, Vermont. The succeeding three years saw the Rutland operating on a profitable basis, as construction materials for the St. Lawrence Seaway were handled. The road also benefitted from a diversion of traffic due to this project. The red ink resumed in 1959, while operating employees continued to be dissatisfied with the Rutland's wage structure. A 41-day strike began on September 16, 1960, and while operations resumed in November, a strike one year later would lead to the road's abandonment.

B. L. Stone photo

ILLINOIS CENTRAL NO. 1152

Exchange near 77th, Chicago, Illinois | 1955

Electrification of Illinois Central suburban services was required as part of the Chicago Lake Front Ordinance of 1919, which also sought to restrict development along the lakefront. Illinois Central quickly moved to the forefront of commuter railroads, operating a rapid transit-like service for decades. At the time of this 1955 photo, the base period service on the South Chicago Branch saw four-car trains operating on a 20-minute headway. The 1950s were tough on the neighborhood—10 percent of South Chicago's population moved out in that decade, and the succeeding decades would lead to further decline as U.S. Steel's South Works and other major employers closed their facilities. The apartment building to the right of the IC train still stands. Even the base for the crossing gateman's shanty is intact at Exchange and 77th. Illinois Central's original multiple-unit cars from 1926 were replaced by successive orders of new cars during the 1970s.

R. V. Mehlenbeck photo

PHILADELPHIA TRANSPORTATION CO. NO. 8215

Market and Front, Philadelphia, Pennsylvania | circa 1955

Originally called High Street, what would later become Philadelphia's Market Street was built on an expansive right-of-way to host the city's many market stalls. Today's name was commonly applied to this thoroughfare by 1800. You can get a feel for the street's considerable width in this view that looks west on Market from Front Street, circa 1955. Philadelphia Transportation Company's (by then under National City Lines control) Peter Witt-style car 8215 is operating on the South 17th-18th Street lines, which was converted to bus on December 29, 1957. Philadelphia Transportation Company had ordered 535 of the 8000-series Peter Witt-style cars and 135 of the 5000-class double-end cars in 1923. The order was first reported in the *Electric Railway Journal* of March 10, 1923. A little over three months later, the first completed cars of both configurations were illustrated and described in the *Journal.*

C. Houser photo

DEPARTMENT OF STREET RAILWAYS NO. 188

Michigan and Woodward, Detroit, Michigan | April 17, 1955

1955 was the last year in which the Department of Street Railways car 188 would run in Detroit. Here, it approaches Michigan and Woodward working the Michigan-Gratiot through route, which had been in effect since November 1950. To the left is the 1871 city hall with one of the 14 sandstone maidens standing guard. Never cleaned, demolition of city hall began in the dark of night on August 14, 1961. At right is Daniel Burnham's Beaux-Arts-style Majestic Building of 1896. The Majestic closed in 1961 and was replaced by the First Federal Building in 1965. As for the PCC car, new to DSR in August 1949, it was one of 183 PCCs (out of 186 total in Detroit) that were sold to Mexico City in October 1955, becoming its car 2188. Cars not sold to Mexico City included two prewar cars and one wrecked all-electric car.

W. C. Janssen photo

133

NEW YORK CITY TRANSIT AUTHORITY NO. 1080

Sea Breeze near Ocean Parkway, Brooklyn, New York | October 21, 1955

Brooklyn & Queens Transit received the first of its PCC cars in August 1936, and revenue service with the new cars began two months later. Brooklyn & Queens Transit found that the greater carrying capacity and higher speeds the PCCs could attain led to a 31 percent increase in revenues, while increasing car-miles by only 4 percent. Based on these results, it's no surprise that B&QT wanted to buy more of the streamliners. However, these plans were scuttled due to the city takeover of B&QT operations on June 1, 1940.

Under the New York City Board of Transportation, the cars began to be repainted in the green and silver scheme that car 1080 wears in this October 21, 1955, view at the Sea Breeze-Ocean Parkway terminal. A highway construction project would end rail service on the 68 line at the end of the following month.

Krambles-Peterson Archive

MISSOURI PACIFIC FA2 NO. 382

Jefferson City, Missouri | circa 1956

The Missouri River and the 1917-vintage state capitol building dominate this view at the Missouri Pacific's Jefferson City Yard, circa 1956. Coincidentally, this was the year that the MP emerged from its 23-year receivership, a record in the rail industry. Missouri Pacific had amassed a fleet of 141 Alco FA1/FB1, FA2/FB2, and FPA2 locomotives as part of its postwar dieselization. The No. 382, one of 43 FA2s, wears a grimy version of the dark cerulean, icterine yellow, and isabelline gray *Eagle* image. This attractive scheme and the survival of the FAs would both fall victim to Downing B. Jenks' management of the MP from 1961. John German (ex-Great Northern) became the MP's chief mechanical officer under Jenks and a program of mechanical department simplification and cost reduction led to a decision to eliminate the FAs, FBs, and FPAs. A handful of FAs survived into the 1962 renumbering program; most of the others donated their trucks and other components to MP's large fleet of GP18s.

G. M. Sebree photo

MONTREAL TRANSPORTATION COMMISSION NO. 2174

St. Catherine-Peel, Montreal, Quebec | circa 1956

St. Catherine Street was already a hub of commercial activity in Montreal when horsecars began operating on it in 1864. Electrified in 1892, the line received the city's first "Pay-As-You-Enter" cars from mid-1904. In addition to being the city's major shopping thoroughfare, St. Catherine was also a key route around Mt. Royal. This resulted in heavy ridership and high turnover of passengers in both directions of travel throughout the operating day. For the Montreal Street Railway and its successor Transportation Commission (from 1951), it meant that the traffic demands of St. Catherine went a long way toward shaping the design and equipping of new rolling stock. This was certainly the case with 140 lightweight two-man cars bought in the late '20s. No. 2174, one of 30 cars from the 1928 Canadian Car & Foundry order, is westbound at Peel Street. St. Catherine was converted to bus operation in early September 1956.

J. W. Vigrass photo

New York, Ontario & Western Caboose No. 8341 and FT No. 807

Norwich, New York | circa 1956

At one time, the New York, Ontario & Western had derived 50 percent of its income from hauling anthracite coal. Decline in coal usage, a shift of manufacturing activities, and movement of population away from the area the railroad served drove the carrier into bankruptcy in 1937, from which it would never emerge. The road experienced a 63 percent reduction in ton-miles between 1944 and 1956, when Electro-Motive Division FT No. 807 and caboose 8341 were photographed in Norwich, N.Y. This view looks east across the north end of NYO&W's facility in the town. The building in the background was part of the Norwich Knitting factory. Today, parking lots occupy the land where the engine house and yard once sat, while farther to the south a high school sits on the former railyard location. Midland Drive, running on the west side of the redeveloped land, commemorates NYO&W's Midland Railroad predecessor.

Krambles-Peterson Archive

SAN FRANCISCO MUNICIPAL RAILWAYS NO. 121

Geary and Van Ness, San Francisco, California | circa 1956

There was nothing subtle about Tommy's Joynt, inside or out. The restaurant is still in this location, shorn of the upper floors and all those great bay windows, sadly. San Francisco Municipal Railways' B, C, and D lines ran past the restaurant on Geary Street, as Type B number 121 is doing in this 1956 view. December 29, 1956, marked the end of rail service on Geary, which had been the Muni's first route, superseding the Geary cable car line on December 28, 1912. A few years prior to this shot, Muni's H-Potrero line cars would have run left to right across this view on Van Ness Street.

Tommy's was family owned from 1947 until 2015, when the family sold the building and the restaurant operation. Conditions of the sale included that the name had to remain unchanged, employees had to be retained (many have worked there for 30 to 40 years) and retention of the union local that represented the employees had to be maintained.

J. R. Williams photo

143

SPERRY RAIL SERVICE No. 130

Belmar, New Jersey | November 1956

The need to test rails for internal defects was determined in the wake of an August 1911 accident on the Lehigh Valley near Manchester, N.Y. Ultimately, the U.S. Bureau of Standards determined that a broken rail had caused this accident. It would take several years to find a practical method for inspecting rails to isolate internal defects. Finally, in 1923, Dr. Elmer Sperry developed the induction system for testing rails. The first of many familiar rail detector cars ran on the Wabash in 1928. By the late '30s, a fleet of 10 such cars was in operation. In this November 1956 photo, an ex-Lehigh Valley motorcar is inspecting the New York & Long Branch around 13th Street in Belmar, N.J. Belmar holds a place in popular culture—E Street in Belmar provided the name for Bruce Springsteen's band, while its harbor was the home port for Tony Soprano's boat, the *Stugots*.

S. D. Maguire photo

New York Central S-2 No. 102

Mott Haven Yard, New York, New York | June 1957

That Chicago, Burlington & Quincy sleeper cut in ahead of the observation car tells us this is the *Commodore Vanderbilt* consist being switched at Mott Haven Yard in June 1957. The era of the transcontinental sleepers and the *Commodore* were both coming to an end. The Central briefly discontinued the train during August 1957 but reinstated it in September. However, in late October, the through car via the *Commodore* to the *California Zephyr* would be discontinued, leaving only the New York-Los Angeles through cars (using the *City of Los Angeles*) in its consist. Coaches were added to the *Commodore* to allow the *Pacemaker* to be dropped from the "Great Steel Fleet." In late April 1958, the *Commodore* was combined with the *Century*, and the extra fare was dropped. On October 30, 1960, the *Commodore* disappeared from the NYC timetable altogether. Members of the NYC's S-Motor class would remain in service for successor Penn Central into the 1970s.

T. H. Desnoyers photo

Belfast & Moosehead Lake
GE 70-ton No. 50

Depot Street, Unity, Maine | July 1957

The 33-mile Belfast & Moosehead Lake was built between 1868 and 1870. Construction was complicated by the track gauge to be used, as the Maine Central (to which the B&ML connected at Burnham Junction) was in the process of standard-gauging. Majority ownership of the line was held by the city of Belfast, which leased the line to the Maine Central for operating responsibility. Dieselization began in 1946 with the delivery of two GE 70-ton units that November, just nine months after the railroad's board had authorized their purchase. Labor and fuel savings due to the new locomotives were quickly realized, and the pair were paid off in mid-1950. A third GE (No. 52) was bought during 1951. Traffic data for a 15-day period in the spring of 1957 shows that two eastbound freights were being run on a typical day, with an average length of five cars. The loss of bulk milk haulage for H.P. Hood & Sons in April 1959 was a heavy blow to the short line. Belfast & Moosehead Lake 50 is picking up a milk car at the Hood Creamery on Depot Street in Unity, Maine.

B. L. Stone photo

149

CANADIAN NATIONAL NO. 5056

Ottawa Union Station, Ottawa, Ontario | circa July 1957

The Mackenzie King Bridge (named for Canada's three-term prime minister) provides the vantage point for the action at Ottawa Union Station circa July 1957. Canadian National steam was in eclipse—238 locomotives had been retired in 1955, an additional 192 left the roster during 1956, and 263 would be retired in 1957. The 1957 total included CN Class J-3-B 5056, which would wrap up a 44-year operating career. This engine had been built by Montreal Locomotive Works for the Grand Trunk Railway, which opened its new station in Ottawa in 1912. When Canadian Pacific closed its Broad Street Station in 1920 and moved its trains to the CN facility, it truly became a Union Station. The July 31, 1966, departure of CN's *Panorama* at 12:40 a.m. brought Union Station's rail use to a close. Canadian National and CP (and later, VIA) operations were moved to a new facility about 2 miles southwest of this center-city location. The old station building remains in use as a Federal Conference Center, while the Nicholas Expressway and Colonel By Drive now run on the former rail right-of-way.

J. W. Vigrass photo

151

TORONTO TRANSIT COMMISSION NO. 4653

Bloor and Yonge, Toronto, Ontario | July 5, 1957

Taking advantage of the Independence Day holiday in the United States, Bob Mehlenbeck made a trip to Canadian interurban and streetcar systems in July 1957. The afternoon rush is in full swing on Toronto's Bloor-Danforth line with 3 two-car trains visible in this view near Yonge Street. Headways on the west end were as little as every 129 seconds, but as intense as this operation was, the east end saw multiple-car trains running on a 90-second headway. A total of 55 two-car trains were operated out of the Danforth and Lansdowne car houses to deliver the required service. Train service on this route had begun on March 13, 1950. Toronto's considerable second-hand PCC purchases dramatically modernized its multiple-unit car fleet. Approaching the photographer, No. 4653 is one of the ex-Cleveland Pullman-built cars of 1946 that TTC acquired in 1952. This car had received couplers in 1954.

R. V. Mehlenbeck photo

153

Ottawa Transportation Commission No. 1001

Sparks and Connor, Ottawa, Ontario | July 6, 1957

Despite the modern appearance (new carbodies were provided in 1947 by Ottawa Car Co.), the four cars in the Ottawa Electric Railway's 1001-series rode on second-hand trucks and used an outdated braking system. Ottawa Transportation Commission had bought four sets of Brill 77E trucks from the Third Avenue Railway, and the brake equipment was salvaged from the recently closed Hull Electric Railway. Use of this obsolete equipment made the cars slow to respond to the operator's actions, meaning they were not operator favorites.

The city bought OER's operation in 1950. Car 1001 is shown westbound on Sparks at O'Connor on July 6, 1957. These cars were retired on January 12, 1959, when the Bank Line was converted. The last streetcars in Ottawa ran on the Britannia Route, which operated until May 1, 1959. Sparks became pedestrian-only during the summer from 1960, and in 1967, it was permanently made into a pedestrian mall.

R. V. Mehlenbeck photo

ERIE LITERARY STREET YARD

Cleveland, Ohio | circa February 1958

University Road in Cleveland provides the overlook for this early 1958 view of the hub of activity that the Erie Railroad's Literary Street Yard then represented. A wide array of homeroad and interchange freight cars make up the foreground with various industrial valley concentrations driving all this activity. One of U.S. Steel's many ore-hauling ships is docked on the Cuyahoga River with mountains of iron ore ready to be fed along with coke and limestone into the nearby blast furnaces. By the 1950s, 14,000 workers were employed in Cleveland's many steel plants, making this second only to auto production in the region. Today, only the red brick and concrete tower to the left of this view still stands, along with a scattering of buildings along West Third Street. The Erie line is just a scar on the earth through here, heading to the former Erie dock.

W. A. McCaleb photo

157

PITTSBURGH RAILWAYS CO. NO. 1287

Liberty and Wood, Pittsburgh, Pennsylvania | May 30, 1958

Pittsburgh Railways air-electric PCC 1287 is shown eastbound on Liberty Avenue near Wood in this May 1958 view. This section of Liberty Avenue had seen its up-and-down cycles over time. The area would later become famous as Pittsburgh's Red Light District in the 1970s and '80s. In fact, the Pittsburgh Cultural Trust, formed in 1984, had the specific mission of turning the area into a cultural district. The 200-seat Art Cinema dated to 1931, when, as the Avenue Cinema, it showed artistic films. It doesn't take much imagination to guess what was shown there in the district's Red Light days. Today, it does business as the Harris Theater. Dimling's Candy store is actually an Art Deco false-front, which was later removed and revealed the Greek-Revival-style facades of the two 19th century buildings behind it. Dimling's went out of business in 1969, and a now-departed massage parlor occupied the site for a while.

W. C. Janssen photo

158

PENNSYLVANIA RAILROAD GG1 NO. 4932

Harrison, New Jersey | September 9, 1958

Pennsy control of the Lehigh Valley began with PRR's acquisition of Delaware & Hudson's 30 percent ownership share in the late '20s. Ultimately, Pennsy would hold 85 percent of the LV shares. Since 1918, LV passenger trains had operated to/from Penn Station, New York, when the United States Railroad Administration granted them access to the terminal. This included the *Black Diamond Express*, which had begun operating in mid-May 1896. In later years, operated simply as the *Black Diamond*, the train was the pride of the road, which marketed itself as The Route of the Black Diamond. By this September 1958 view at Harrison, N.J., the *Diamond's* days were numbered. The *Asa Packer* had been discontinued the previous April, which led LV to shift the *Diamond* to an earlier departure time from New York City. Heading toward the PRR-LV connection at Waverly Avenue, Newark, the *Diamond* would run for less than one more year, with its final trips being made on May 11, 1959.

G. Krambles photo

161

SOUTHERN PACIFIC F7 NO. 6190

La Puente, California | March 10, 1959

Southern Pacific F7 No. 6190 heads Train 4, the eastbound *Golden State*, at La Puente on March 10, 1959. La Puente had been settled in the 1840s, but the city was not incorporated until August 1, 1956. Although the days of matched red-and-silver E7s and the extra-fare 1948 *Golden State* consist are gone, this was still a formidable train. Most days it still ran to 14 cars, 10 of which were destined for Chicago, two to Kansas City, and two to Minneapolis. Kansas City-destined cars included one head-end car and a coach. Through Minneapolis equipment comprised one coach and one 8-roomette, 6-double-bedroom sleeper. Equipment making the 2,200-plus-mile trek to Chicago included two sleepers, a grille-lounge, bar-lounge, a diner, three coaches, a baggage-dorm and an RPO-baggage. A greatly diminished *Golden State* would make its final run in February 1968.

Krambles-Peterson Archive

Richmond, Fredericksburg & Potomac E8 No. 1006

Ninth Street, Washington, D.C. | June 25, 1960

This June 25, 1960, view looks west from Washington's Ninth Street North East bridge over the Ivy City Yard. Washington Terminal RS1s go about their switching jobs and a set of RF&P passenger power is on the move. Tracks on the bridge are the connection between the Baltimore & Ohio's Metropolitan Subdivision and the road's Washington Subdivision. Before the turn of the century, this location had been the site of the Ivy City fairgrounds/race track. Construction of the rail yard (to support Union Station development) began in 1907. The railroad's investment led to a considerable improvement of infrastructure in the neighborhood, and these improvements made possible the extensive industrial development in Ivy City from the 1930s. Richmond, Fredericksburg & Potomac acquired 20 E8s between 1949 and 1953. No. 1006 was part of its second order and wore a February 1952 builder's date. After its RF&P career, it ran as Amtrak 216 and later as No. 439.

E. Miller photo

CHICAGO GREAT WESTERN F3 NO. 113C

Forest Park, Illinois | July 1960

Chicago Great Western was late to the party in most of the markets it served, rewarding it with a longer or less-desirable routing than the competition. This section of the line through Forest Park, Ill. (as seen from the Desplaines Avenue L station) was completed by 1887 and relied on a Baltimore & Ohio Chicago Terminal connection to reach downtown Chicago and to make connections with other area rail carriers. Chicago Great Western had the longest route between Chicago and Kansas City (33 percent longer than the Santa Fe) and in the Chicago-Omaha market, only the Illinois Central's route was longer than CGW's. These disadvantages meant CGW had to be resourceful. In the steam era, it bought 2-10-4s to handle its famous long freights, and the road was an early proponent of trailer-on-flatcar (from 1936). By the time of this July 1960 view, CGW was hauling 2.474 million net ton miles of freight annually.

J. W. Vigrass photo

DELAWARE, LACKAWANNA & WESTERN NO. 2543

Montclair, New Jersey | October 13, 1960

Lackawanna service to West Bloomfield (later, Montclair) was begun in June 1856 by predecessor Newark & Bloomfield. That road was acquired by the Morris & Essex in 1868, and although the M&E was not dissolved until July 1945, service to/from Montclair was conducted by the Lackawanna for the next 90 years. Double-tracking and grade-separation of the Montclair line was undertaken in 1912. A new six-track terminal in Montclair was built in 1913.

Five days before the merger with the Erie was to take effect (October 17, 1960) Johnnie Williams shot this midday train at the station. Though the terminal facility was replaced in 1981, the Grecian-Doric-styled station-house has survived through adaptive reuse. The former DL&W MU cars ran for the last time on August 24, 1984; New Jersey Transit had taken over responsibility for the suburban services the previous year. In 2002, NJ Transit built the Montclair connection to tie the ex-Erie Boonton Line to the former Lackawanna Montclair Branch.

J. R. Williams photo

NEW ORLEANS PUBLIC SERVICE INC. NO. 943

Canal and Carondolet, New Orleans, Louisiana | January 1, 1961

A drainage ditch in the central business district (admittedly filled in by 1866) gave New Orleans's great transit thoroughfare its name. The canal and horsecar service (provided by New Orleans City Railroad) co-existed for five years. Electric cars took over on Canal in 1894. By 1922, New Orleans Public Service had assumed operating responsibility for the system, and the Beeler Organization was commissioned to study the operation in detail. For example, separate looping tracks for the Bourbon and Carondolet lines had been recommended to improve the flow of all services. This view from New Year's Day 1961 shows Canal and Carondolet several decades later. Separating the flow of the car lines allowed the Canal through tracks to handle up to 95 cars per hour per track without interference from the 40 cars per hour on the Carondolet-St. Charles service. Another aspect addressed was the acquisition of 173 new steel, double-truck cars from Brill and Perley-Thomas. No. 843 was part of that Perley-Thomas order. Buses took over on Canal on May 31, 1964.

J. R. Williams photo

MISSOURI & ILLINOIS BRIDGE & BELT 44-TON NO. 100

Henry Street, Alton, Illinois | February 25, 1961

In almost two decades of production, General Electric delivered 334 44-ton locomotives to domestic customers. The majority (93 percent) were equipped with a pair of Caterpillar D17000 8-cylinder prime movers. Missouri & Illinois Bridge & Belt 100, produced within the first year of 44-tonner construction, was part of that majority. Missouri & Illinois Bridge & Belt operated a 3-mile rail line via the Alton Bridge connecting Alton, Ill., to West Alton, Mo. Originally owned by a group of mainline carriers, similar to the nearby Terminal Railroad Association of St. Louis, the M&IB&B eventually passed to sole control under the Chicago, Burlington & Quincy, explaining the livery depicted in this photo. No. 100 is shown eastbound at Henry Street in Alton in February 1961. Later repainted in Illinois Terminal colors, the 100 was wrecked after a collision with an Illinois Terminal freight. M&IB&B was dissolved in 1966. The structure to the left of the Frisco boxcar is the old Clark Bridge to West Alton, dating to 1928. This was replaced by a cable-stayed bridge, which opened in 1994.

Krambles-Peterson Archive

172

BALTIMORE TRANSIT NO. 7116

Fayette Street, Baltimore, Maryland | circa May 1961

Just half a year after this photo, on November 3, 1963, Baltimore Transit would end streetcar service on its No. 8 and 15 lines responding to pressure from the city government to make Fayette Street a one-way thoroughfare. The two cars are westbound on Fayette at Howard Street. PCC operation (and for a while, BTC's one Brilliner) on the 8 line had begun in 1939, while the 15 line first received PCC cars from 1941. Head car 7116 is part of a 1944 Pullman order. BTC ordered only prewar PCCs and this 1944 order would be their last.

Today, Howard Street is the route of Baltimore's light rail line through the downtown area. The buildings on the north side of Fayette, behind the streetcars, have survived (albeit in a currently sad state). The newer building down the block (beyond the Trailways Depot) was cleared. The successor transit agency, the Maryland Mass Transit Administration, still routes line 8 and 15 buses past this location.

G. H. Landau photo

ERIE-LACKAWANNA FA1 No. 7304

Crain Avenue, Kent, Ohio | June 1961

Erie-Lackawanna westbound through freights working the yard in Kent, Ohio, were usually confined to late night and pre-dawn periods. Alco FA1 No. 7304 heads the SC-99 from Scranton to Chicago as it crosses Crain Avenue in Kent in June 1961. This train's designation conforms to the Erie practice, though E-L would also run symbol freights that followed the DL&W system using low numbers in combination with alpha descriptors. Erie-Lackawanna was hit hard by the opening of the St. Lawrence Seaway; while ton-miles were on the increase throughout E-L's first decade (reaching their peak in 1969), car loadings were slowly eroding. Erie-Lackawanna steadily lost money, posting an operating profit only in 1965–66 and 1969. The former E-L line through Kent has been reduced to a single-track today (operated by the Akron-Barberton Cluster Railway), paralleling the 10-mile Portage Hike and Bike Trail.

J. W. Vigrass photo

Chicago North Shore & Milwaukee 801-class

40th and Indiana, Chicago, Illinois | June 25, 1961

North Shore Line secured trackage rights over the L as far south as Roosevelt Road in Chicago from August 1919. By mid-February 1922, passenger trains were operating to and from 63rd-Dorchester on the Jackson Park Branch, and for a while, Merchandise Despatch trains were using the L's 63rd Lower Yard (just east of Calumet Avenue). A late-depression era economy saw North Shore service cut back to Roosevelt Road. The cutback also facilitated the connection at the south end of the new State Street Subway to the south side L. A June 25, 1961, Central Electric Railfans' Association charter trip took the *Electroliner* to otherwise-unfamiliar surroundings. In this instance, the vantage point is the pedestrian bridge of the 40th-Indiana station. Typical south side apartments and factories make up most of the background, but the new construction at the center-top of the photo is one of the Stateway Gardens (public housing) high-rises. Eventually comprising six 17-story and two 10-story buildings, this complex, which had once been home to 3,000 residents, was demolished between 2000 and 2006.

J. J. Buckley photo

SYDNEY & LOUISBOURG NO. 85

Glace Bay, Nova Scotia | July 25, 1961

As late as 1955, the Sydney & Louisbourg Railway was still acquiring second-hand steam. In March of that year, S&L had received two locomotives each from the Chicago & Illinois Midland and the Pittsburgh & Lake Erie, as well as a single engine from the Detroit & Toledo Shore Line. No. 85, shown in this July 1961 view, was an earlier acquisition from the D&TSL, having been built by Alco in 1925 as D&TSL No. 110. Even in May 1961, it was still possible to see eight to ten active steam locomotives each day on the S&L, but diesels were making their inroads. Yellow chevron stripes in the gap between No. 85 and the mixed-train's combine belong to one of seven RS1s the S&L had bought from the Soo (Wisconsin Central) and the Minneapolis & St. Louis to dieselize. The last active steam on the S&L ran on November 20, 1961, although disposition of the locomotives extended for several years.

J. W. Vigrass photo

DC Transit No. 1526

Sixth and Pennsylvania, Washington, D.C | circa 1962

Capital Traction amassed a fleet of 489 St. Louis-built PCCs in a series of orders placed between 1937 and 1946. Between 30 and 67 cars were included in the orders placed each year from 1937 to 1942. Subsequent orders of 65, 75, and 50 cars were placed in the 1944–1946 period. All orders split the provision of electrical equipment between General Electric and Westinghouse. Car 1526, one of the GE-equipped cars from the 1945 order, is shown southbound on Sixth at Pennsylvania. In 1963, the 1526 was one of 46 cars sold to Tranvias de Barcelona, where it became No. 1640. It remained active in Barcelona until 1969. If you look immediately above the red awning to the left of the PCC, you'll see the words Coast Line in the stone. This Atlantic Coast Line building dates to 1892–93. The building still stands, having been integrated into a newer structure in 1991.

Krambles-Peterson Archive

SOUTHERN PACIFIC AS-616 NO. 5239

Alameda Street, Los Angeles, California | March 1962

Southern Pacific crews used to call the area on the east side of downtown Los Angeles the rat hole. This section of Alameda Street near Ord is adjacent to Chinatown, the historic Phillippe (The Original) restaurant, and the Los Angeles Union Passenger Terminal. The main track ran down the center of Alameda, but there were numerous sidings and spurs. Santa Fe and Union Pacific also once had considerable in-street operations in Los Angeles. Southern Pacific had an extensive warehouse complex at Seventh and Alameda—the buildings were familiar from the many television shows or movies that included them. The former SP trackage was removed between First and Seventh Streets in 2012, although south of Seventh, it was still intact into 2017. Southern Pacific Baldwin AS-616 No. 5239 shown in this March 1962 view was sold to the Oregon & North Western in 1964. Although later preserved, the locomotive was parted-out and scrapped in 2009.

Krambles-Peterson Archive

LOS ANGELES METROPOLITAN TRANSIT AUTHORITY NO. 3148

First and Broadway, Los Angeles, California | February 11, 1963

Los Angeles Railway opened the Pico-East First streetcar line in 1895. Subsequently extended, the line adopted the P designation in 1920. Operation under LARy, and later Los Angeles Transit Lines (following National City Lines' 1945 takeover), passed to the Los Angeles Metropolitan Transit Authority in 1958. Wearing LAMTA's two-tone-green and white scheme, postwar PCC 3148 heads from northbound Broadway onto eastbound First Street in February 1963. Los Angeles Metropolitan Transit Authority will rid itself of the five remaining streetcar lines and its two trolleybus routes in just over a month's time on March 31, 1963. No. 3148 was a celebrity in its own right: in February 1960, the car was re-trucked using standard gauge PCC trucks borrowed from the San Francisco Municipal Railway and operated in test service on the former Pacific Electric line to Watts. Following the end of streetcar service, this car was sold for continued use in Cairo, Egypt.

W. C. Janssen photo

187

NORTHERN PACIFIC NW2 NO. 102 AND SOO AS-16 NO. 380

Fourth Avenue, Minneapolis, Minnesota | March 1963

Following the Civil War, Minneapolis became a concentration of both rail lines and wholesale distribution, which logically led to a warehouse district being created near the city's central area. The bulk of this activity was located to the north of Hennepin Avenue and east of Washington Avenue, although there was also a pocket of warehouse activity along the rail corridor on the west side of Washington. This activity exploded in the 20th century, extending up both sides of Washington to 10th Avenue North and filling in between and around the areas of 19th century warehouse development. In terms of economic activity, where in 1880 wholesale trade had totaled $24 million, by 1919 it was valued at $1 billion. Many architectural styles are evident in this March 1963 view at Fourth Avenue North, including Italianate, Queen Anne, Richardsonian Romanesque, and Classic Revival styles

S. Baker photo

189

READING COMPANY H24-66 NO. 862

Harrisburg, Pennsylvania | March 15, 1963

The Reading's first taste of Fairbanks-Morse diesel power came with the December 31, 1939, delivery of a 600 hp centercab switcher, which eventually became Reading No. 97. It ran until 1953 when it was traded in on the first batch of Train Masters for the Reading. Nine units were built in late 1953, followed by an additional six in late 1955, including No. 862 shown in Harrisburg on March 15, 1963. A final pair came at the end of 1956, for a total of 17 units of this model.

No. 862 and train are waiting on the 4:05 p.m. departure time of Train 194. Harrisburg-Allentown service was still provided on a seven-days-per-week basis, although train names officially hadn't been applied to these services for a decade. The white building behind the TOFC cars served as Reading's freight and passenger station until the June 30, 1963, discontinuance of the passenger train.

A. Holtz photo

CHICAGO SOUTH SHORE & SOUTH BEND NO. 110

LaSalle Street, South Bend, Indiana | July 5, 1963

South Shore Line 110 (a 1951 rebuild of coach 10 from the 1929 Standard Steel car order) rests after dropping the last of its passengers at LaSalle and Michigan in South Bend on Friday, July 5, 1963. The timetable in effect at this time scheduled 19 trains to South Bend and 18 return trips, with the last of these leaving for Chicago at 10:55 p.m. Chesapeake & Ohio acquired the South Shore in January 1967, and by late October, service to/from South Bend had been reduced to 11 round trips. The road received permission to abandon its in-street trackage in South Bend and cut back service to a station at Bendix (alongside the Penn Central, ex-New York Central Chicago line) in July 1970. The South Shore timetable that went into effect in June 1972 showed just three eastbounds to Bendix and only two departures from that station each day.

J. W. Vigrass photo

LONG ISLAND RAIL ROAD NO. 2528

Kew Gardens, Queens, New York | April 21, 1965

New York Central's 1962 Pullman-Standard MU car order was the basis for the design of Long Island's 30-car "Zip Car" order of 1963. Twelve 2500-series motor cars, including the 2528 shown here heading a southbound train at Kew Gardens, were included, with the balance being 2600-series trailers. This car still wears the full World's Fair lettering for the 1964–65 event, which was served by a special station on the Port Washington Branch. The huge Budd-built M1-series car order replaced these cars in multiple-unit service from 1973, after which they were used in locomotive-hauled trains. Kew Gardens is on the LIRR main line, just under 2 miles from Jamaica and slightly less than 10 miles to Penn Station. This section of line was electrified in 1910. On November 22, 1950, Kew Gardens (then in the boundaries of Richmond Hills) was the site of a tragic rear-end collision, which resulted in 78 deaths and 363 injuries.

G. Krambles photo

PENNSYLVANIA RAILROAD NO. 267

20th Street, Philadelphia, Pennsylvania | September 22, 1965

The Pennsy opened Suburban Station in Philadelphia on September 28, 1930. Earlier in the year, the PRR had moved its offices from Broad Street Station into the office building above the new, seven-track terminal, later called One Penn Center. By the early '50s, Suburban Station had been expanded to a 10-track facility (originally designed for 12 tracks), allowing Broad Street to be closed on April 27, 1952. The 2.2 percent grade on the climb to 30th Street Station (a Silverliner MU train is shown at 20th Street on the ramp in September 1965) is the reason PRR chose not to move the Clockers or the Atlantic City trains to Suburban Station. A deal for the development of the Penn Center complex, on the site of Broad Street Station, was signed in May 1953. Office towers and a Sheraton Hotel were among the first buildings included in this development. In January 1957, the Pennsy's main offices were moved to the 6 Penn Center building.

T. H. Desnoyers photo

El Paso City Lines No. 1513

San Antonio Street, El Paso, Texas | July 1966

To modernize its international streetcar line, El Paso City Lines acquired 20 of the 28 PCCs built for San Diego Electric Railway in 1937–38. The last day for San Diego streetcars was April 24, 1949. Sale of the first 17 cars was completed in early 1950, with the balance heading to El Paso in late 1952. Former San Diego car 520 (part of the 1937 order from St. Louis Car Company) became El Paso City Lines 1513. National City Lines had owned the El Paso property from 1943. Retention of streetcars on the international car line was due to two factors—it continued to be a profitable operation, and the company did not have the authority to run buses in Mexico. Operation of the international line ended on September 4, 1974. No. 1513 is a survivor, currently being rebuilt by Brookville to serve on El Paso's new 4.8-mile trolley line that recently opened.

R. W. Gibson photo

WESTERN PACIFIC F7 NO. 804D

Third and Washington, Oakland, California | 1968

The first spike on Western Pacific Railway's Oakland extension was driven on January 2, 1906, at Third and Union, less than a mile west of this 1968 shot at the WP's Oakland station. Up to that time, the Southern Pacific had a stranglehold on access to the Oakland waterfront. On the night of January 5, 1906, the WP's track was built on rock quays installed to prevent silt from washing into the harbor. This effectively meant SP's track no longer marked the waterfront, allowing the city to regain control of the waterfront. Western Pacific's extension opened for freight service in December 1909, with passenger service commencing the following August. The high cost to build the WP, along with the impacts of the 1907 depression, forced the WP into bankruptcy in 1916. Reorganized in 1917, the road would again seek protection in 1935, re-emerging as the Western Pacific Railroad in 1945.

G. M. Sebree photo

PHILADELPHIA TRANSPORTATION CO. NO. 2778

10th and Erie, Philadelphia, Pennsylvania | January 23, 1968

With Philadelphia Transportation's Luzerne Car House just three blocks to the north of this scene at 10th and Erie Streets, 10th is full of afternoon pull-out cars for January 23, 1968's evening rush. Luzerne had opened as an operating location in 1913 and originally could accommodate up to 470 streetcars in a combination of covered storage and open-air yards. In the 1950s, PTC had begun operating buses out of Luzerne as some rail lines were converted. The 56/Erie-Torresdale was one of six rail routes Luzerne served in early 1968; there were also 15 bus lines operating out of this facility. Southeastern Pennsylvania Transportation Authority took possession of PTC operations on September 30, 1968. Car 2778, heading the pull-out parade, had been delivered to PTC in April 1947. SEPTA scrapped the car in 1983. Rail service on Erie-Torresdale was suspended in June of 1992. Luzerne ceased to be an operating location in April 1997.

T. H. Desnoyers photo

203

BURLINGTON NORTHERN F9 NO. 836

Lyndale Avenue, Minneapolis, Minnesota | February 21, 1971

In the post-Conrail merger period, they became known as "patch jobs," as predecessor road names, logos, and numbers were covered over. By contrast, the Burlington Northern roster consolidation process proceeded with amazing order and the results could be termed graceful by comparison. Just a year into the merger, an all ex-NP consist leads a westbound train at Lyndale Avenue, Minneapolis. Northern Pacific rostered more F9s than any other road (71 total) and three from different orders are in this consist. The ex-NP F9s were long-lived, with many running for 26 to 28 years. Conversely, the trailing unit of this consist, ex-NP U28C 2809, was active for just 15 years. Today, Lyndale Junction sees about 17 trains per day routed via the BNSF Monticello or Wayzata Subdivisions. The ex-Minneapolis & St. Louis/Chicago & North Western line past this location is now a bike trail. Union Pacific has trackage rights over the BNSF to access its Golden Valley Industrial Lead (the former Minnesota Western).

Krambles-Peterson Archive

Baltimore & Ohio GP40 No. 4040

Camden Station, Baltimore, Maryland | circa June 1972

Construction of the 1.4-mile tunnel under Howard Street in Baltimore occurred between 1890 and 1895. Electrified operation began in 1895, using an overhead contact line for power distribution. This arrangement was superseded by use of a third rail through the tunnel circa 1902. Clearances were always an issue, leading to construction of a gantlet track to handle higher and wider loads in 1937. With the third-rail electrification still in use, locomotives were equipped with a swing-out contact shoe that was used to draw current from either of the original tracks when running on the gantlet. Dieselization superseded electric-hauled trains through the tunnel in 1952. Under CSX operation, the tunnel has experienced a major train derailment/fire (in July 2001) and a retaining wall collapse (April 2014). Increased clearances for double-stack trains, etc., remain an issue for CSX. Baltimore & Ohio Electro-Motive Division GP40 4040, one of 161 on the B&O roster, leads a southbound train past Camden Station around June 1972.

Krambles-Peterson Archive

CHICAGO, ROCK ISLAND & PACIFIC *BIG BEN*

Roosevelt Road, Chicago, Illinois | June 14, 1973

I had a soft spot for the Rock out of all proportion to its relative importance. It didn't hurt that it ran right past the Illinois Institute of Technology campus, where it provided a pleasant diversion to thermodynamics or partial-differential equations. General Electric U25Bs with mis-matched hood doors, cabs, and noses added to the attraction; that, plus the chance to catch Alco C415s working around town exerted their pull. It was painful to watch the Rock in decline, as exemplified by its Quad Cities and Peoria trains. The ex-*Golden State* cars had been transferred to these services on discontinuance of the transcontinental service in 1968. To stimulate patronage, the Rock lowered fares that same year. Ex-Rio Grande dome-observation car *Big Ben* joined the Butterworth Tours fleet in 1971 and provided a finishing touch to the Quad Cities trains. Dining car service persisted until 1976, thanks to a union contract obligation. The end for the Rock's intercity trains finally came on January 1, 1979.

Art Peterson photo

BURLINGTON NORTHERN F7 NO. 9736

Techny, Illinois | December 21, 1973

Not all cityscapes undergo a graceful transition. Rural land is being given an industrial makeover in this December 21, 1973, view at Techny, Ill. (between Glenview and Northbrook) as a late-running Amtrak Train 8, the *Empire Builder,* kicks up a snowstorm in its wake. To the general public, Techny might be known for housing the headquarters of the Divine Word Missionary, but just west of that complex was Tower B-20 on the Milwaukee Road North Line, where the Milwaukee connected with the freight-only Chicago & North Western "New Line." The vantage point is the C&NW lattice through-truss bridge over the Milwaukee main line. Milwaukee freights had trackage rights over the C&NW for 10 miles to access their owner's Bensenville Yards. Amtrak's "rainbow era" was still in full swing, though time was running out for lead F7 BN 9736—she would be traded in to Precision National eight months later.

Art Peterson photo

ATCHISON, TOPEKA & SANTA FE S2 NO. 2389

Roosevelt Road, Chicago, Illinois | circa 1973-74

Alco executives attempted to carry over a small-batch, custom-production focus into their diesel production techniques. The longtime locomotive manufacturer failed to adjust its corporate culture to respond to technological changes. It was not until 1952 that Alco selected a chief executive with considerable diesel engine experience. This failure to capitalize on the dieselization trend is even more disappointing considering that Alco owned McIntosh & Seymour, a well-established engine manufacturer, from 1929.

Despite these challenges, Alco did enjoy some successes. The best-selling locomotive in its catalog was the 1,000 hp model S2 switcher, of which 1,502 were built between 1940 and 1950. These locomotives used the M&S model 539-T engine produced in Auburn, N.Y. Santa Fe had the third largest group of S2s totaling 70 locomotives. The 2389 was a December 1949 product of the Schenectady factory. It ran until February 1975.

Art Peterson photo

213

DELAWARE & HUDSON U23B NO. 2312

Michigan Central Station, Detroit, Michigan | July 1974

The Delaware & Hudson was the launch customer for General Electric's U23B locomotive, taking delivery of 16 of them in 1968. No. 315 was an early casualty, having left the roster in 1971. The remaining 15 units all made it to the Guilford acquisition and continued to run for that carrier into the mid-'80s. Locomotive 2312 managed to wear six liveries over the course of its D&H career. Selected to head the "Preamble Express" in the summer of 1974, the 2312 wore this striking color combination as the train operated over the proposed route the *American Freedom Train* would later follow. Its route in late July took it from Indianapolis to Detroit and then on to Kalamazoo. A couple of weeks later, Union Pacific E9 951 replaced the 2312 when the *Express* arrived in Omaha and headed the train until it tied up in Baltimore in November 1974.

W. A. McCaleb photo

CHICAGO TRANSIT AUTHORITY NO. 6228

35th and State, Chicago, Illinois | October 3, 1974

No mistaking Chicago's powerful skyline and the dramatic nature of the city as shown in this October 1974 view looking north from the 35th Street L station. This was Chicago's original L line, which celebrated 125 years of service on June 6, 2017. The rising and falling profile of the structure dates to its construction when this feature was incorporated to aid the steam-powered trains on approaching and leaving station locations.

The mix of old and new buildings along with styles ranging from Gothic to Art Deco to Bauhaus to Modernist is evident from west to east in this view which includes (from left to right) Sears (now Willis) Tower, Board of Trade, First National Bank Building, Marina City Towers, United Insurance Building, CNA Building, John Hancock Center, and Standard Oil Building (among others). Immediately to the left of the CTA train is a corner of the Illinois Institute of Technology campus, which was designed by Mies van der Rohe.

Art Peterson photo

NORFOLK & WESTERN GP35 NO. 201

Hohman Avenue, Hammond, Indiana | October 3, 1976

Four "Pevler blue" Geeps, led by GP35 201, head south across Hohman Avenue, Hammond, Ind., on October 3, 1976. Herman H. Pevler had started his rail career with the Pennsy and headed the Wabash from mid-1959 until October 1, 1963, when he became president of the Norfolk & Western. Under Pevler's administration, the N&W "hamburger" logo and the "Pevler blue" livery began to adorn N&W locomotives. Pevler moved into the presidency immediately after Stuart T. Saunders, who had put the N&W's mergers with the Nickel Plate and the Wabash in motion. Post-merger, N&W encompassed nearly 7,600 route-miles and transitioned into a major carrier serving key western markets. From Hammond into Chicago, freight could be routed via either the ex-Nickel Plate to Calumet Yard (at Stony Island and 103rd) or via the former Wabash line to Landers Yard on 79th Street west of Western Avenue.

Art Peterson photo

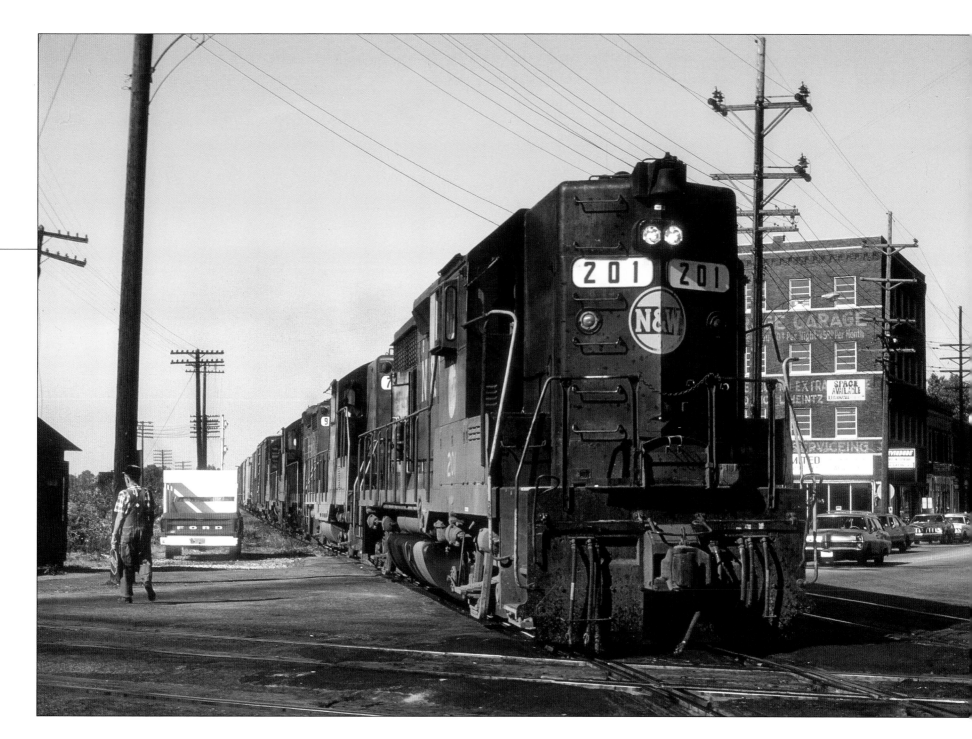

GO TRANSIT FP7 NO. 902

Bathurst Street, Toronto, Ontario | February 11, 1983

Cabin D in Toronto was built by the Grand Trunk Railway in the 1890s. Located at the convergence of the Canadian National Oakville and Weston Subdivisions with the Canadian Pacific Galt Subdivision, and just 1.1 miles west of Toronto Union Station, the location was extremely busy. Expansion of GO Transit's rail operation led to replacement of the flat junction with a fly-under and preservation of Cabin D, which, along with its Saxby & Farmer level plant, was relocated to the nearby Toronto Railway Heritage Center. Train 3028, viewed from the Bathurst Street bridge, is being led by one of 11 auxiliary power/control units GO Transit used to provide head-end power. No. 902 had been built in June of 1952 as Ontario Northland 1507; it was one of four FP7s GO acquired in 1974. Trailing it are six of the 123-car fleet of Hawker Siddeley-built single-level passenger cars GO once rostered.

Art Peterson photo

ACKNOWLEDGEMENTS

My thanks to the folks, publications, and institutions listed below for their help in researching the subject matter of the images included in this book. Any errors or omissions are entirely my fault!

Eli Bail

Bernard Craig

Electric Railway Journal

Phil Gosney

Blaine Hays

Tom Hunter

George Kanary

Greg Kennelly

Bill Lipsman

Louis Marre

Angus McIntyre

Oklahoma Historical Society

PRR Technical & Historical Society

San Francisco Public Library

Ed Skuchas

Larry Thomas

Mike Trosino

Alan Weeks

Wally Young

Rick Bates

Mike Del Vecchio

Bernie Feltman

Herb Harwood

Bill Howes

Dave Ingles

Walter Keevil

Lyle Key

Dave Lotz

Courtney McCormick

Steve McKay

Jeff Otto

Rick Powell

Fred W. Schneider III

Greg Sommers

Tom Thornhill

Bill Vigrass

Mike Weinman

Canadian Rail

Otto Dobnick

Jack Ferry

Steve Haworth

Stan Hunter

Dale Jenkins

Bill Kemp

Kiplinger Library

Ed Lybarger

Rob McGonigal

Bruce C. Nelson

Joe Papay

Henry Raudenbush

Cliff Scholes

Charlie Sullivan

"Tommy's Joynt"

Bill Volkmer

Ted Wickson

Two people who need to be singled-out for special recognition are my uncle, George Krambles, and my wife, Tina Peterson. George gave me the education of a lifetime in the business, as well as showing me how to strike a balance between a career and fandom. As for Tina, she has shown infinite patience with "this thing of mine." Whether it meant sitting patiently waiting for a train to show, or enduring my noticeably faster driving when trying to get ahead of a train, she has suffered through it all in way better humor than I had any right to expect.

Lastly, I'd be remiss if I didn't acknowledge the considerable skill and efforts of my editors at Kalmbach Media—Randy Rehberg, Eric White, and Jeff Wilson—and designer Lisa Bergman.

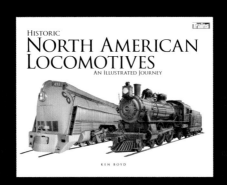
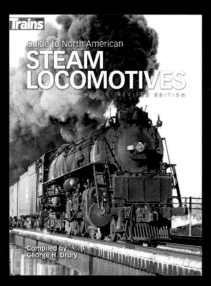
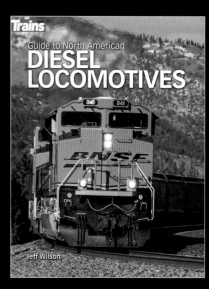
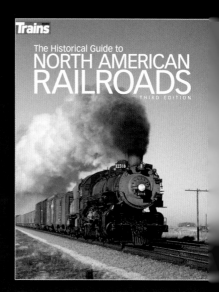